9 3/4

LEGO Harry Potter

IDEAS BOOK

WRITTEN BY HANNAH DOLAN
AND JULIA MARCH

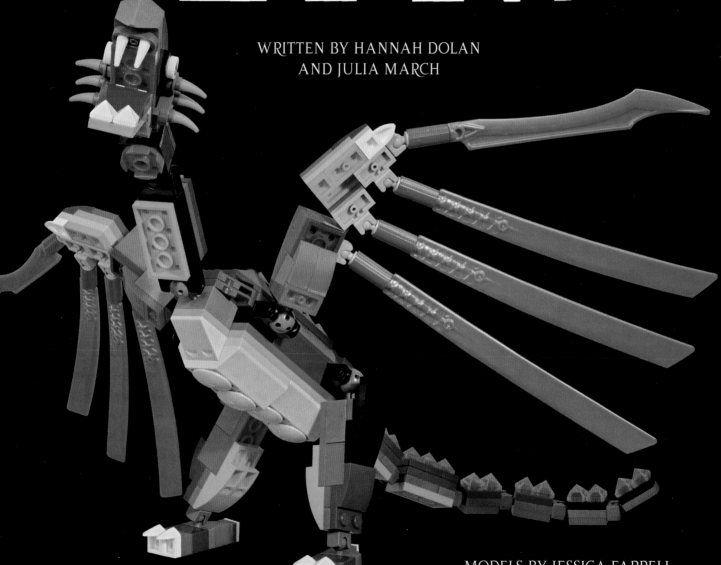

MODELS BY JESSICA FARRELL,
ALEXANDER BLAIS, ROD GILLIES, BARNEY MAIN,
MARIANN ASANUMA, AND NATE DIAS

CONTENTS

Spot Padfoot on page 54

MOVIE MOMENTS 64

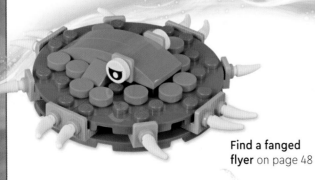

Find a fanged flyer on page 48

Get organized on page 132

Play your cards right on page 184

INTRODUCTION

The wondrous world of Harry Potter is filled with unusual items and amazing moments. This book shows you how to make many of them and more, with no magic wands required! Gather your LEGO® bricks, muster your imagination, and prepare for a spellbinding building adventure. Here are some things to think about before you begin.

MOMENTS

Get in among the action by recalling memorable events, fierce battles, or touching moments in the Harry Potter stories. Let them inspire your most magical models, whether they're objects, scenes, or games.

BE HARRY POTTER INSPIRED

Immerse yourself in all things Harry Potter to power your creativity. Watch the films, read the books, and look at LEGO sets to inspire you and help you remember specific things you love.

CHARACTERS

Take inspiration from your favorite witch, wizard, Muggle, or creature and build their LEGO likenesses. You could also build parts of their costume or objects they own or use.

LOCATIONS

Study the buildings, caves, streets, and forests of Harry Potter's world to help you decide how to depict them in LEGO pieces. Think about the architectural styles, landscapes, and atmospheres of locations you want to build.

EXPAND THE WORLD

Don't be limited by what you can already see in Harry Potter's world. You could build things that have never been unearthed or looked at closely before. Create new objects, scenes, or games to put your own spin on the spellbinding universe.

COLOR AND CHARACTER

Consider the color palettes and design styles of Harry Potter's world so your models will look in keeping with it. The buildings and landscapes are often ancient and familiar with a magical twist. Find pieces in your collection that will create the right feel.

BUILDER TIPS

Feeling ready to build a Harry Potter creation? Here are some tips to help you start thinking like a builder as well as a witch or wizard. For more expert advice, turn to the "Meet the builders" section at the back of the book (pages 188–195).

WHERE TO START?

PICK A TECHNIQUE

You could base your model design around a particular building technique you want to try, such a sideways building or creating a round shape. There are many different building techniques in this book—why not choose one to try out?

FOCUS ON FIGURES OR PIECES

You can let your LEGO® pieces and figures lead the way in helping you decide what to build. Are the colors or shapes of your pieces just right for a particular model, or do you want to build something for one of your minifigures?

I WILL RULE OVER ALL YOUR OTHER MINIFIGURES!

PLAN IT OUT...

Once you have an idea for a model, try drawing it out or describing it in words. If you're more technologically minded, you could plan out your model on computer programs like LEGO Digital Designer or BrickLink Studio. They let you design LEGO models digitally using a huge library of pieces.

...OR JUST BUILD

Some people don't like to plan out their models to any degree—they just start clicking pieces together and see where they end up. This kind of free building allows you to decide what you're creating as you build it. If you don't like what you've built initially, just start again!

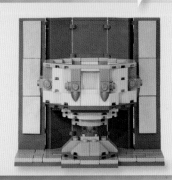

TOP TIPS

CONSIDER SCALE

Decide on the scale you want to build from the start. If you're building something that minifigures can sit, play, or live inside, that's minifigure scale. Anything smaller than that is microscale. You may also want to build something bigger than minifigure scale, such as the life-size quills opposite.

LIFE SIZE

MICROSCALE   **MINIFIGURE SCALE**

PLAY WITH COLORS

If you don't have lots of pieces in the perfect color, combine a mix of hues or have fun making something a completely different color than usual.

MEASURE YOUR MINIFIGURES

If you want minifigures to sit or stand inside your models, think about your minifigures' dimensions and how they'll attach or fit inside. Make sure they have enough space for their arms, legs, and head.

GET ORGANIZED

Sort some of your LEGO collection into element types and colors before you begin. This way you won't spend lots of time searching for particular pieces as you build.

POTTER PARTY

Arrange a Harry Potter-themed building session with family and friends to enhance the joy of building. You can share your favorite magical moments as well as building knowledge and ideas.

WHAT'S THAT POTTER?

WATCH AND PLAY

Why not put on one of the Harry Potter films while you build, then make some of the interesting things you see?

CHAPTER ONE

MAGICAL OBJECTS

From potent potion ingredients to pesky pixie playmates... there must be many magical bits and pieces you've seen in the Harry Potter movies that you'd love to get your hands on. Here's a bubbling brew of brick-built magical objects to satisfy any witch or wizard.

SHOPPING IN DIAGON ALLEY

If a student of magic has some Galleons to spend, they might take their purse on a shopping spree in Diagon Alley—a cobbled lane tucked away in London and totally invisible to Muggles. It's jam-packed with wizarding shops selling all kinds of magical items to inspire your builds.

6×12 plate book-cover base

SIDE VIEW

2×2 curved slopes angle down to the spine

1×3 curved slopes for the page ends

Tan pieces are well-thumbed pages

OPEN THE BOOK

Spell books are a top seller at Flourish and Blotts, the popular book store. Diaries, history books, and biographies are in demand, too. This open book's blank pages could be printed in invisible ink! You could incorporate black pieces to look like text.

TELESCOPE

Any students interested in astronomy set their trajectory toward Twinkle's Telescopes, which specializes in star-gazing maps and devices. This antique-looking handheld device should fit neatly inside a wizard's cloak pocket.

LEGO® Technic pin holds the finderscope in place

2×2 round bricks for the eyepiece

2×2 slide plate lens

SPECIAL PIECE

The round brick in the middle of the telescope has four useful holes around its circumference. These holes can be used to attach extra details via LEGO Technic pins.

Attach a star plate for a mystical look

4×4 round bricks and 2×2 macaroni bricks form the main tube

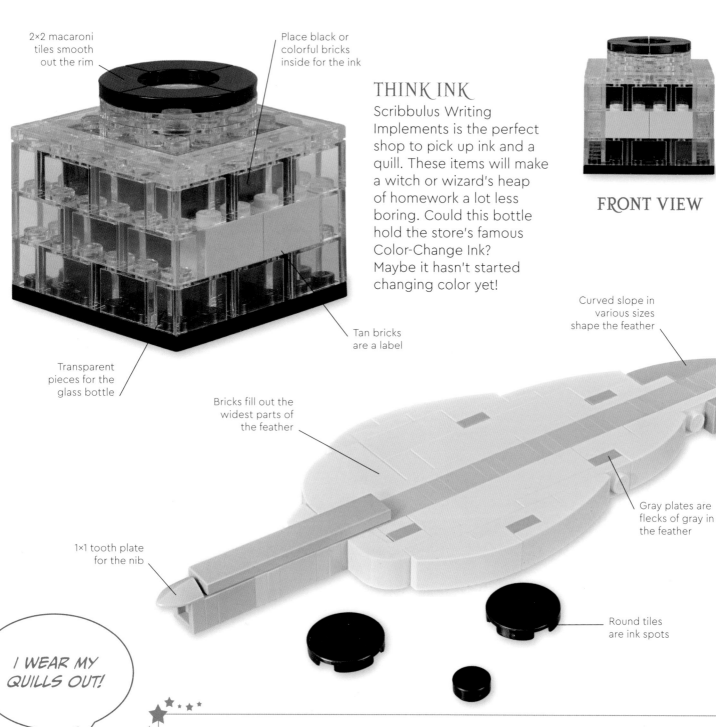

2×2 macaroni tiles smooth out the rim

Place black or colorful bricks inside for the ink

THINK INK

Scribbulus Writing Implements is the perfect shop to pick up ink and a quill. These items will make a witch or wizard's heap of homework a lot less boring. Could this bottle hold the store's famous Color-Change Ink? Maybe it hasn't started changing color yet!

FRONT VIEW

Tan bricks are a label

Transparent pieces for the glass bottle

Curved slope in various sizes shape the feather

Bricks fill out the widest parts of the feather

Gray plates are flecks of gray in the feather

1×1 tooth plate for the nib

Round tiles are ink spots

I WEAR MY QUILLS OUT!

PARTS OF A FEATHER

The quill's snowy white feather has a central shaft made from small plates and bricks with studs on two sides. The two white sections of the feather attach sideways to this shaft.

1×1 brick with side studs on opposite sides

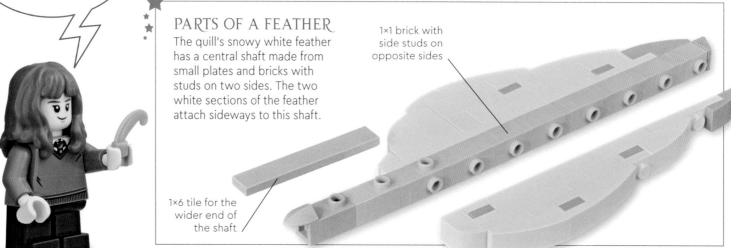

1×6 tile for the wider end of the shaft

PACKING FOR HOGWARTS

For their first term at Hogwarts, a witch or wizard will require a roomy trunk filled with everything they might need, including books, inks, and potions, as well as slightly less magical necessities like socks. Build them what they need, and don't forget their Hogwarts acceptance letter—otherwise they might get turned away at the door.

BUILD TIP

The trunk design mixes two shades of brown so its texture looks like well-traveled leather. Mix and play with colors to get the right texture for your builds.

Handles either side are plates with bars

Gray 1×1 tile looks like a metal clasp

Lid opens up on a clip-and-bar connection

Potions shelf fits neatly inside

Tiles line the rim so the lid lifts easily

INSIDE VIEW

Lots of tiles attached sideways form the trunk's front side

I'LL NEED MAGIC TO LIFT THIS TRUNK.

ROOM IN THE TRUNK

Make sure the trunk is big enough to fit every item in. If not, you'll just have to rebuild it to the correct size. If only there was a real-life size-changing spell! Give it strong handles and a secure clasp.

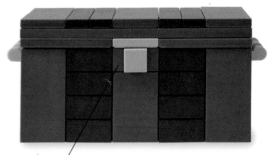

1×2 jumper plate holds the clasp

FRONT VIEW

This plume of feathers is a tiny quill

PACK IT IN

Students must arrive prepared for their first magic lesson with some spell books and potions. They may also need a cozy pair of socks for chilly nights in a dorm room.

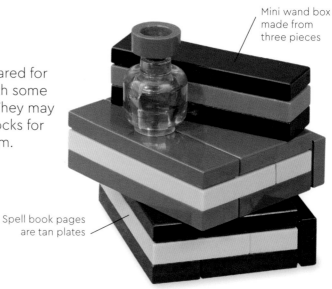

Mini wand box made from three pieces

Black pieces look like an ink pot

Spell book pages are tan plates

SPELL BOOKS

Two rows of bricks form the back of the shelf

1×1 round tiles with bars top the potion bottles

POTIONS SHELF

1×2 rounded plate fits below the sock's heel and toe

SOCK

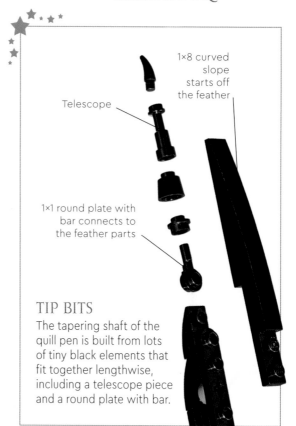

1×8 curved slope starts off the feather

Telescope

1×1 round plate with bar connects to the feather parts

TIP BITS

The tapering shaft of the quill pen is built from lots of tiny black elements that fit together lengthwise, including a telescope piece and a round plate with bar.

WISHFUL INKING

This quill and ink pot is a life-size build, so it won't fit inside the trunk opposite. But it's the perfect size for writing out a list of items to pack for Hogwarts.

Small round plates add flecks of gray

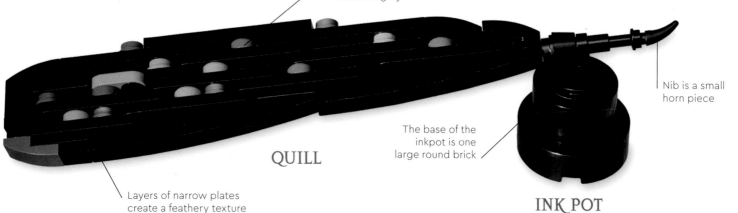

Nib is a small horn piece

The base of the inkpot is one large round brick

QUILL

Layers of narrow plates create a feathery texture

INK POT

TROLLEY TREATS

Most students get hungry on the long train ride to Hogwarts. Luckily the trolley witch is around, selling treats from her cart, the Honeydukes Express. Take inspiration from the movies to build these trolley treats, or magic up some goodies of your own. But remember, these treats may look tasty but you should never, ever try to eat them!

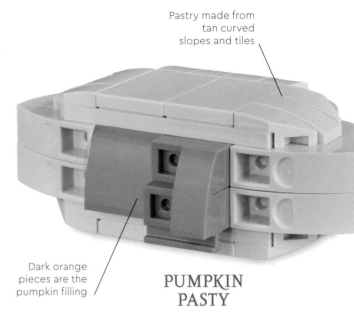

Pastry made from tan curved slopes and tiles

Dark orange pieces are the pumpkin filling

PUMPKIN PASTY

1×2/1×4 bracket plates shape the lid's edges

Four 2×2×1 corner panels form a square

Crazyberry-flavored bubblegum is a 2×2 dome

TREAT OR TRICK?

These are not your average sweets. Chocolate Frogs might hop away, and a bubble blown with Drooble's Best Blowing Gum can't be popped. And good luck to any witch or wizard who chooses Bertie Bott's Every Flavour Beans. They might get an earwax-flavored one!

DROOBLE'S BEST BLOWING GUM

Four 1×1 double curved slopes form a smooth handle

SEEN MY PUMPKIN PASTY, SCABBERS?

Make a wand shape from thin tiles and plates

LICORICE WANDS

2×2 radar dish rounds off the swirly cream topping

These cakes are often served in a stack

CAULDRON BOTTOM

Cauldron cakes are baked at the base of a cauldron so give yours a rounded bottom, then fill your cakes with whatever you like. The 4×4 round plates inside this cake look like zesty lemon curd.

1×1 round plate fits under the radar dish

3×3×1 round corner brick

Two stacked 4×4 round plates

2×2 inverted slope brick

CAULDRON CAKES

This shade of brown looks like milk chocolate

Brown pieces are a charred chocolate base

The bar on this 1×1 rounded plate is a webbed foot

CHOCOLATE FROG

1×1 plate with swirl tops off the lid

Slope bricks form the box lid

1×4×3 transparent panels let you look inside

ANYTHING OFF THE TROLLEY, DEARS?

BERTIE BOTT'S EVERY FLAVOR BEAN

Could this green bean be sprout flavored?

SCHOOL CRESTS

Two schools of magic; two different crests. The Hogwarts crest is divided into four houses, suggesting that fairness is valued. The fancy crest of Beauxbatons' Academy puts an emphasis on elegance. The third famous school of magic, Durmstrang Institute, teaches the Dark Arts. Find and build the crest for that one, too... if you dare.

BEAUXBATONS'

Golden leaves surround the crest of Beauxbatons' Academy, and a flamboyant "B" sits in the middle. It's clear that this French school of magic values all things stylish. Even the half-giant headmistress, Madame Maxime, is super stylish.

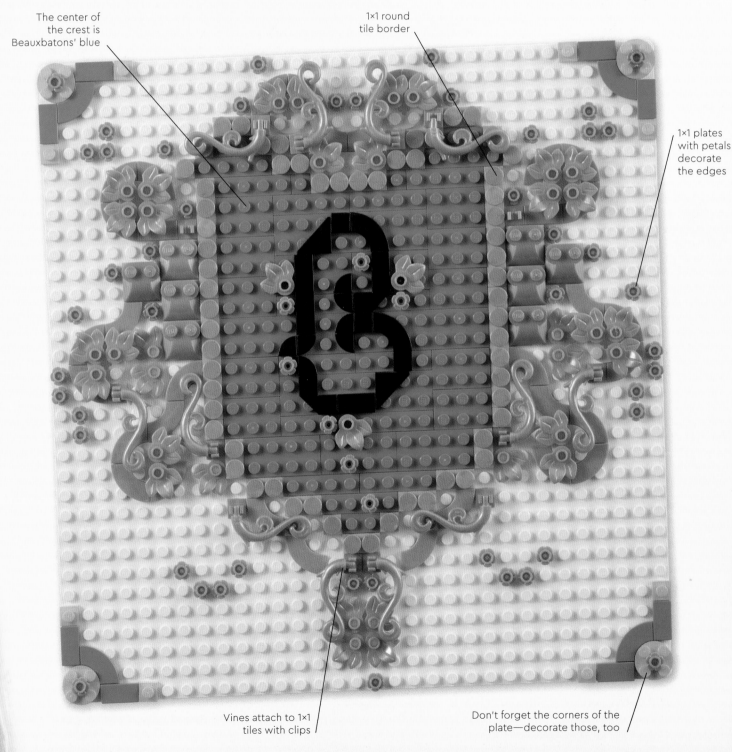

The center of the crest is Beauxbatons' blue

1×1 round tile border

1×1 plates with petals decorate the edges

Vines attach to 1×1 tiles with clips

Don't forget the corners of the plate—decorate those, too

Gray tiles are silver details

1×1 round tiles create serpent emblem

Gold 1×2 tiles divide up the Hogwarts houses

Flame yellow plates create the crest's outline

WELCOME TO HOGWARTS, MADAME MAXIME.

BUILD TIP

These crests are built on 32×32 plates. If you don't have that size plate, combine several smaller plates. Just place plates or bricks over the seams to attach them together.

FOUR HOUSES

Each house is given equal prominence on the Hogwarts school crest. This detailed build has the house symbols—a Gryffindor lion, a Slytherin serpent, a Ravenclaw raven, and a Hufflepuff badger—made out of round tiles.

SORTING HAT

What kind of hat has a face, can talk, and lives on a shelf in the office of Hogwarts headmaster, Professor Albus Dumbledore? The Sorting Hat, of course! This magical hat model sorts every new student into one of four Hogwarts houses based on their personality traits.

The slope pieces get smaller toward the tip

FRONT VIEW

MOVING MOUTH

Well-disguised hinge pieces hidden at the back of the hat allow the top of the mouth to move up and down, as if the hat is talking. Smooth tile pieces line the lower lip so the top of the mouth can open easily.

2×2 hinge plate attached to a 1×2 hinge brick

1×1 quarter tile

Pointy tip is a 1×1 slope

CRUMPLED FEATURES

Your LEGO® Sorting Hat will probably be smaller than life size, but you'll still have room for the details. Use different shaped and colored pieces to represent the creases and folds of the hat's facial features.

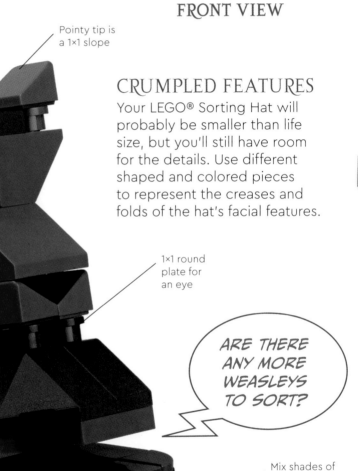

1×1 round plate for an eye

ARE THERE ANY MORE WEASLEYS TO SORT?

Slope bricks placed at right angles create a crumpled effect

Mix shades of brown to highlight the hat's folds

The rim is built around a 6×6 round plate

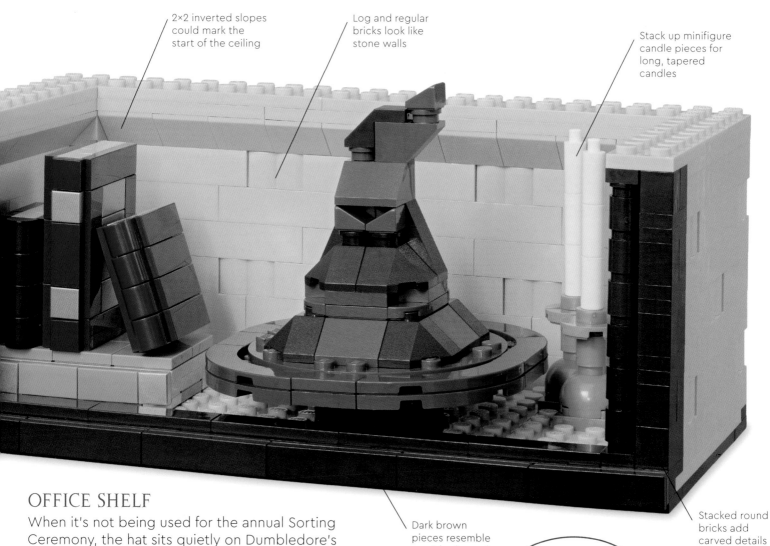

2×2 inverted slopes could mark the start of the ceiling

Log and regular bricks look like stone walls

Stack up minifigure candle pieces for long, tapered candles

OFFICE SHELF

When it's not being used for the annual Sorting Ceremony, the hat sits quietly on Dumbledore's shelf. This model shares the shelf with books and candles, but yours could have potion bottles, trophies, or even a frog or two.

Dark brown pieces resemble varnished wood

Stacked round bricks add carved details

BUILD TIP

The offices of Hogwarts' wise teachers are filled with heavy, academic books. Building details like these into your objects and scenes will bring them to life.

1×1 double curved slopes form this spine

THAT HAT HAS PLENTY OF CHAT!

Tan plates are the dusty pages

STACK OF BOOKS

FOUNDERS' ITEMS

Try building replicas of legendary items created for the founders of Hogwarts. Will you start with Helga Hufflepuff's cup, Salazar Slytherin's locket, Rowena Ravenclaw's diadem, or perhaps Godric Gryffindor's sword? (Look for that one on pages 44–45.) When you've built them all, hide them around your home to be "discovered" later.

BUILD TIP

The upward-shaped curve of the Hufflepuff Cup is made from layers of bricks. To create the shape, make each layer of bricks one stud wider than the last.

Two 1×3 curved slopes shape the handle

Tiles give the cup's rim a smooth finish

Pentagonal tile bears the Hufflepuff crest

HUFFLEPUFF'S CUP

Nobody is quite sure what magic this golden cup contains. Knowing Helga Hufflepuff, it's probably something tasty! Build the cup with a wide, secure base, create two handles, and add the distinctive Hufflepuff crest if you have it.

3×3×2 round corner bricks shape the base

Gold mechanical arms clip onto a 2×2 plate with octagonal bar

I HAVEN'T SEEN THESE OBJECTS FOR YEARS!

FRONT VIEW

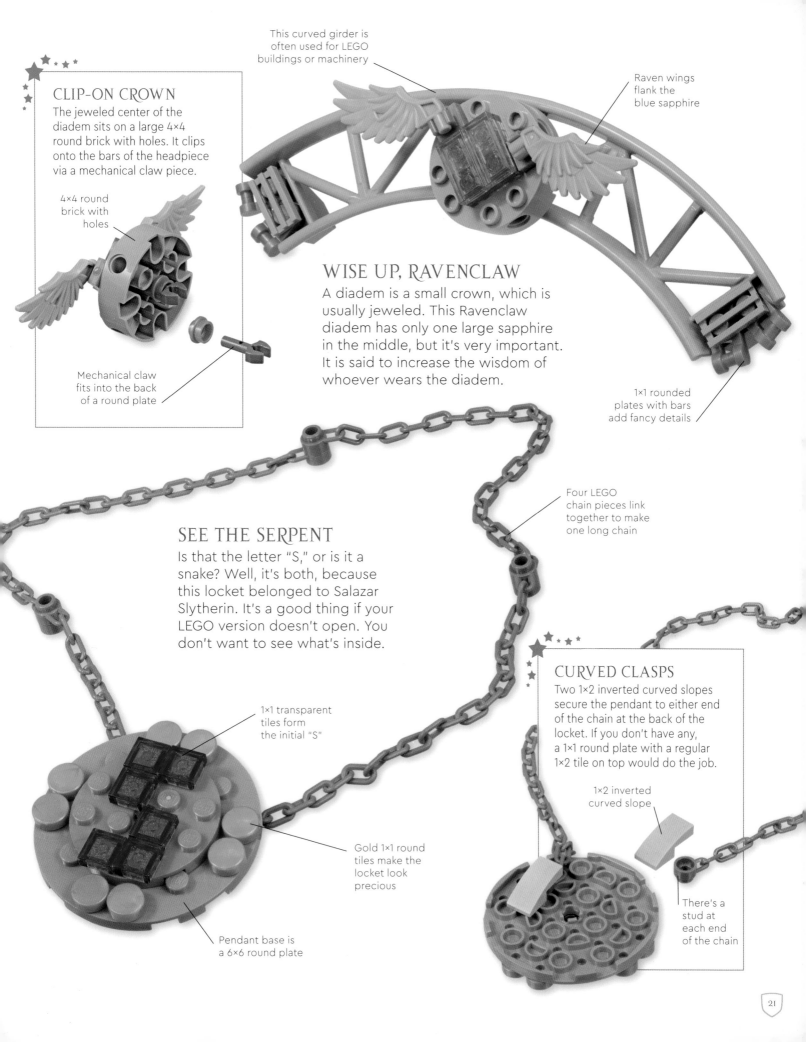

CLIP-ON CROWN

The jeweled center of the diadem sits on a large 4×4 round brick with holes. It clips onto the bars of the headpiece via a mechanical claw piece.

4×4 round brick with holes

Mechanical claw fits into the back of a round plate

This curved girder is often used for LEGO buildings or machinery

Raven wings flank the blue sapphire

WISE UP, RAVENCLAW

A diadem is a small crown, which is usually jeweled. This Ravenclaw diadem has only one large sapphire in the middle, but it's very important. It is said to increase the wisdom of whoever wears the diadem.

1×1 rounded plates with bars add fancy details

Four LEGO chain pieces link together to make one long chain

SEE THE SERPENT

Is that the letter "S," or is it a snake? Well, it's both, because this locket belonged to Salazar Slytherin. It's a good thing if your LEGO version doesn't open. You don't want to see what's inside.

1×1 transparent tiles form the initial "S"

CURVED CLASPS

Two 1×2 inverted curved slopes secure the pendant to either end of the chain at the back of the locket. If you don't have any, a 1×1 round plate with a regular 1×2 tile on top would do the job.

1×2 inverted curved slope

Gold 1×1 round tiles make the locket look precious

Pendant base is a 6×6 round plate

There's a stud at each end of the chain

MOVING PORTRAITS

Have you ever walked past a portrait and felt its eyes were following you? At Hogwarts, that can actually happen. Paintings are enchanted, so they are able to move and talk. These framed portraits have eyes or body parts that can change positions, thanks to a secret mechanism at the back. How could you make a LEGO picture move?

EYE SEE YOU

A hidden slider at the back of this portrait enables this black-hatted wizard to flick his gaze left or right. Watch out, he's looking at you. Or maybe your friend. No, it's definitely you.

Brim of the hat sits at a different level to the middle

Create a wooden frame or a fancy gold or silver one

Narrow tiles and plates for the background

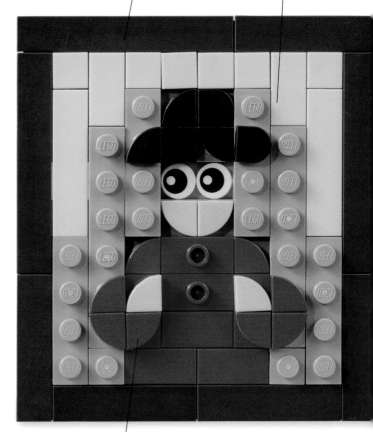

1×1 quarter plates shape the arms and hands

Jumper plate studs look like buttons

SLIDE TO SLIDE

The moving eyes of this portrait attach to a yellow 1×6 plate, which slides in the space between two longer plates. Two black 1×4 tiles with studs fit behind the sliding plate to prevent it from falling out at the back.

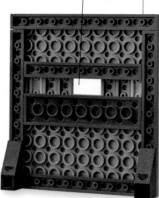

Eyes peek through this hole

1×4 tile with two studs

1×6 plate

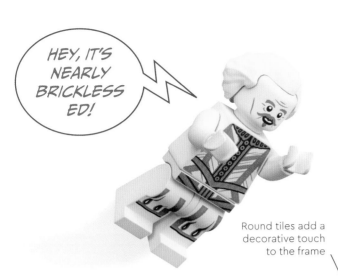

HEY, IT'S NEARLY BRICKLESS ED!

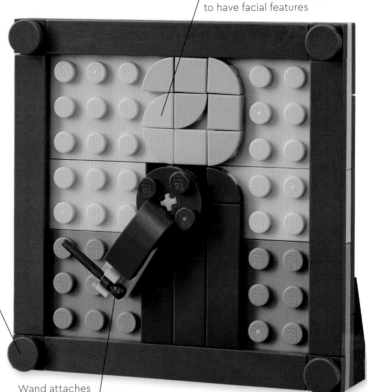

Your portraits don't need to have facial features

Round tiles add a decorative touch to the frame

CATCH THE WAVE

This gray-haired figure is waving his wand... up and down, up and down. He could be casting a spell, or maybe he's just trying to get the attention of his old mate, Gryffindor ghost Nearly Headless Nick. They go back hundreds of years.

Wand attaches to a 1×1 tile with clip

Gray tiles for hair

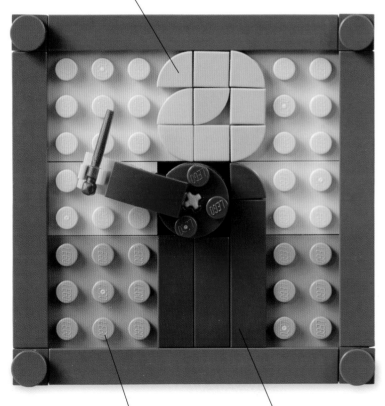

Ball piece attaches to a hidden axle

1×3 inverted slope stand

SIDE VIEW   **REAR VIEW**

SPECIAL PIECE

Can you spot the hidden axle in the wand-waving portrait's shoulder? That piece lets the arm move up and down when the ball is turned at the back of the portrait.

Add more background details or keep it simple

Long, green wizard robes

GREAT HALL FEAST

Imagine an end-of-term blowout in Hogwarts Great Hall. Can you picture the table, filled with hearty roasts, buttered veggies, dainty cakes, and sweet nibbles? They'd all be served up on decorative tableware, of course. Feast your eyes on these LEGO banquet model ideas, then get started building some of your own!

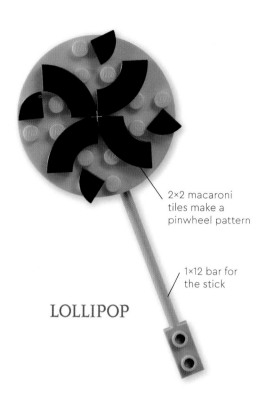

2×2 macaroni tiles make a pinwheel pattern

1×12 bar for the stick

LOLLIPOP

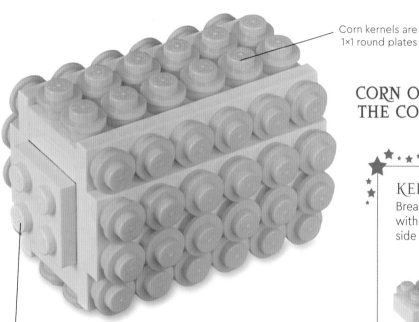

Corn kernels are 1×1 round plates

CORN ON THE COB

The middle and ends of the corn are white like the real thing

FOOD GLORIOUS FOOD

Studs on this chicken leg look like bumpy skin, and yellow round plates create the corn cob. For dessert, colorful lollipops are the perfect accompaniment to lots of cake.

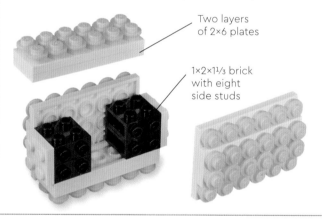

★ ★ · · ★
KERNEL OF TRUTH

Break open the cob and you'll find hardworking bricks with side studs holding the four sides together. Each side is made from one or more layers of white plates.

Two layers of 2×6 plates

1×2×1⅓ brick with eight side studs

YUM!

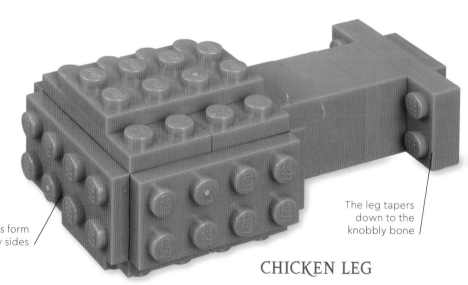

2×4 plates form the meaty sides

The leg tapers down to the knobbly bone

CHICKEN LEG

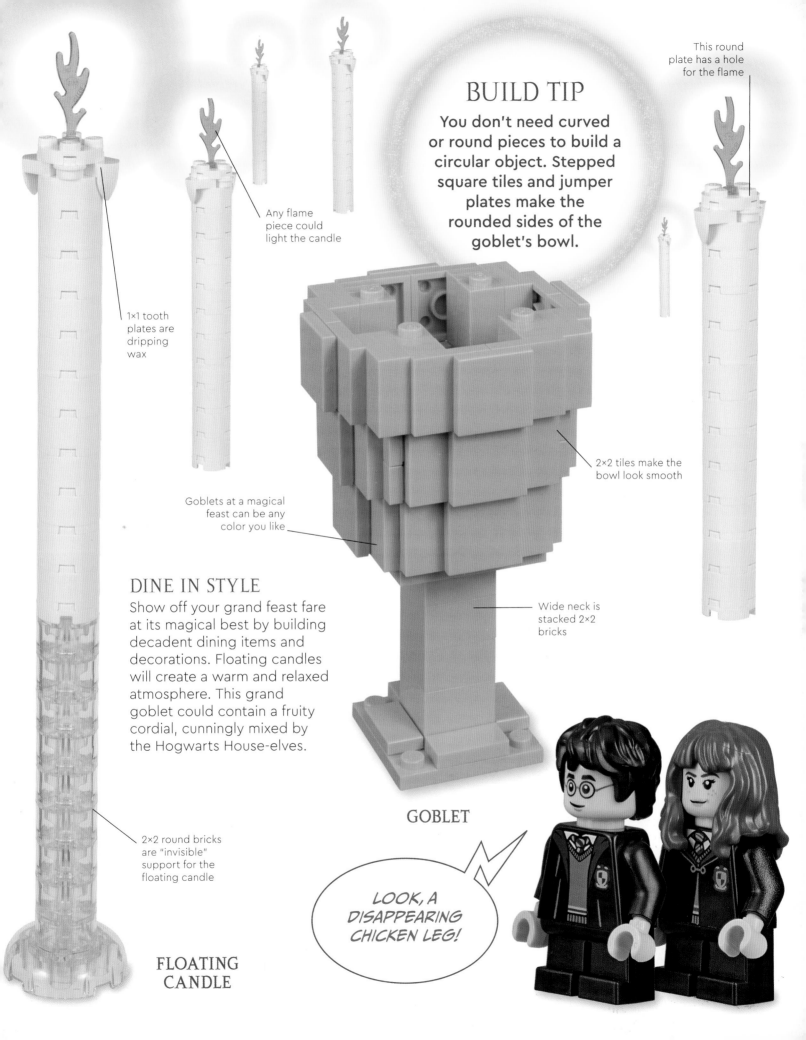

Any flame piece could light the candle

1×1 tooth plates are dripping wax

BUILD TIP

You don't need curved or round pieces to build a circular object. Stepped square tiles and jumper plates make the rounded sides of the goblet's bowl.

This round plate has a hole for the flame

2×2 tiles make the bowl look smooth

Goblets at a magical feast can be any color you like

DINE IN STYLE

Show off your grand feast fare at its magical best by building decadent dining items and decorations. Floating candles will create a warm and relaxed atmosphere. This grand goblet could contain a fruity cordial, cunningly mixed by the Hogwarts House-elves.

Wide neck is stacked 2×2 bricks

GOBLET

2×2 round bricks are "invisible" support for the floating candle

FLOATING CANDLE

LOOK, A DISAPPEARING CHICKEN LEG!

REMEMBRALL AND HOWLER

Hogwarts gets daily deliveries by Owl Post. Try building some of the unusual items delivered by owls. You could create a Remembrall—a magical memory aid. Or shock your friends with a Howler—an angry letter that turns written words into shouts. Be sure to cover your ears if that's your model of choice!

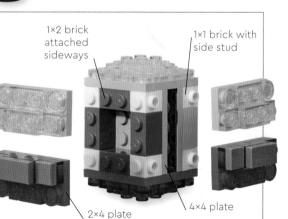

I'LL HIDE THIS FROM NEVILLE. HA, HA!

REMEMBER IT ALL

A Remembrall is a helpful glass ball that alerts the owner when they've forgotten something. Neville Longbottom was sent one at Hogwarts by his gran, but Draco Malfoy took it after Neville crashed his broomstick. Poor Neville would rather forget the whole thing!

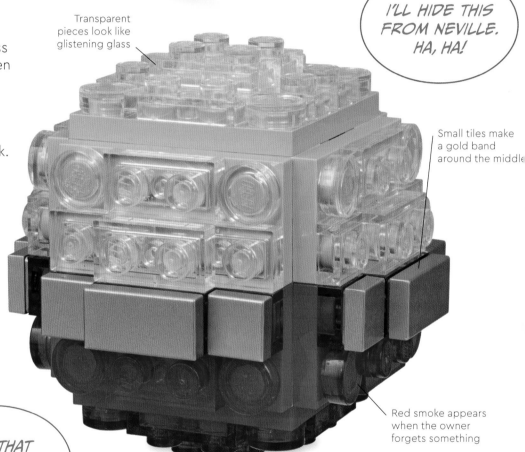

Transparent pieces look like glistening glass

Small tiles make a gold band around the middle

Red smoke appears when the owner forgets something

SIDE VIEW

GIVE THAT BACK TO HIM, MALFOY!

SQUARE START

The ball shape of the Remembrall is built outward from a square. Plates attach to exposed studs on the square, then smaller plates and tiles on top of those plates give the magical object its rounded shape.

1×2 brick attached sideways

1×1 brick with side stud

2×4 plate

4×4 plate

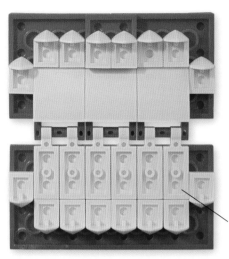

OPEN VIEW
(NO TONGUE)

1×2 plates with clips line the back of the lower jaw

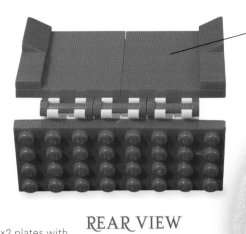

4×4 tile with studs on the edge

REAR VIEW

BUILD TIP
The Howler looks like it's really shouting thanks to moving clips and bars. You could use hinge bricks and plates or click hinge connections to create the same effect.

THE DREADED HOWLER

Oh no... Ron's got a Howler from his mother! Howlers take the form of shouting mouths to deliver their message. Connect some red plates and add sharp teeth and a tongue for a mouth with attitude.

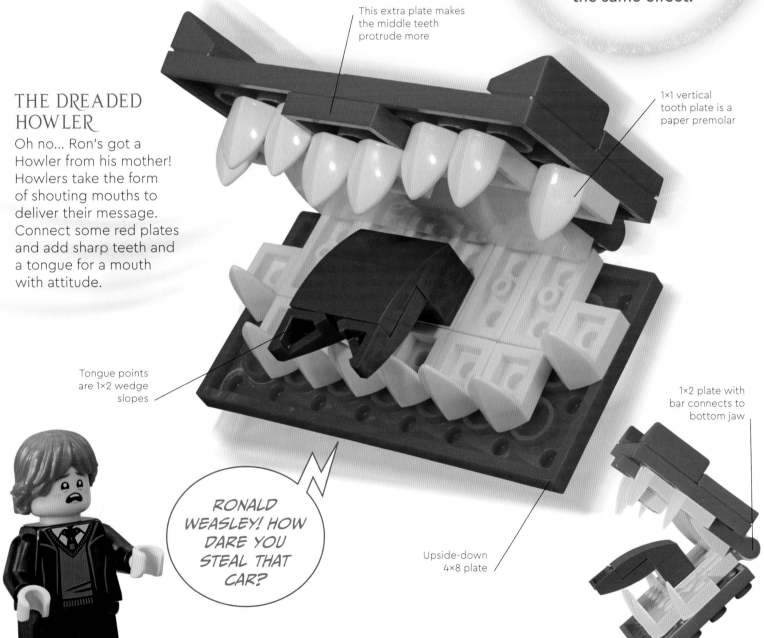

This extra plate makes the middle teeth protrude more

1×1 vertical tooth plate is a paper premolar

Tongue points are 1×2 wedge slopes

1×2 plate with bar connects to bottom jaw

Upside-down 4×8 plate

RONALD WEASLEY! HOW DARE YOU STEAL THAT CAR?

SIDE VIEW

27

POTIONS CLASS

Imagine all the colorful magical ingredients Hogwarts students might see in Professor Severus Snape's Potions Class. Try building some, along with the bottles and tools they might need to mix potions with. Build them well—one potion mishap and students might feel Professor Snape's wrath!

IN THE BALANCE

Magical measuring scales are a must. Getting the quantities of potion ingredients even slightly wrong could result in a potion that turns a student into a hatstand instead of a Quidditch champion.

TIPPING POINT

A 1×12 brick with holes forms the balancing beam of the scales. It swings on a pin that plugs into a smaller 1×2 brick with hole.

1×12 brick with holes

LEGO Technic pin

1×2 brick with hole

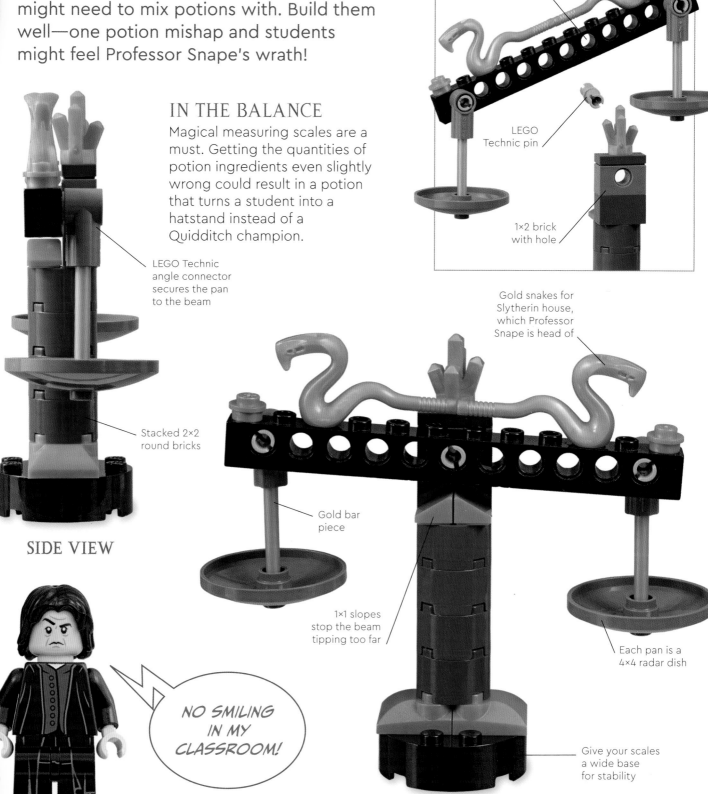

LEGO Technic angle connector secures the pan to the beam

Stacked 2×2 round bricks

SIDE VIEW

Gold snakes for Slytherin house, which Professor Snape is head of

Gold bar piece

1×1 slopes stop the beam tipping too far

Each pan is a 4×4 radar dish

Give your scales a wide base for stability

NO SMILING IN MY CLASSROOM!

Jewel piece is a bottle stopper

Use dome pieces for a curved bottle shape

Connect bottles or flasks with small transparent bricks

Two transparent tiles create the rim

This red brick makes the bottle look half full

INGREDIENTS BOTTLES

You could extend the rack to hold multiple test tubes

BOTTLE IT UP

Show off a rainbow of colored liquids in transparent bottles and test tubes. Why not connect some of the bottles so the ingredients can begin to mix? Stand back...

Arch pieces make a test tube rack

BUILD TIP

The knife's handle is made from two straight angle connectors, but how are they connected? There's a hidden axle piece running between them to make a solid handle.

TEST TUBE AND STAND

4×4 plate base

MAKE THE CUT

Hogwarts students sometimes have to harvest their own herbs, bark, and roots. These can be tough to cut, so build a knife with a good grip and a long blade.

LEGO Technic axle connector

1×1 round plate with open stud

Blade is a minifigure's sword

COOKING POTIONS

Once students have mixed their potions, it's time to get cooking. They can heat up herbals in a sturdy cauldron, a fiery oven, or over a blazing Bunsen burner. You can almost smell the potions as they bubble, hiss, and fill the Hogwarts classroom with fumes. Yum! (Or maybe yuk!)

2×2 macaroni brick

2×2 inverted slope brick

4×4 round plate

LAYER IT UP

Build the cauldron up in layers from a 4×4 round plate base. Inverted slope bricks make the next layer, followed by wedge plates. Macaroni bricks give the cauldron its rounded rim at the top.

Swirly plant stem looks like rising vapors

Bubbling potion is lots of 1×1 round plates

Smooth tiles line the rim of the pot

Gold handle is a 1×2 plate with bar

STIRRING THE POT

A cauldron is a metal pot for cooking over an open fire. It's great for potions where the ingredients must be stirred in gradually. Make sure yours has handles for holding onto when it's hot.

The cauldron stands on three small horn legs

ALL THE INGREDIENTS

Almost anything can be used in some potion or another. Prized ingredients vary from fragrant Anjelica to yucky Bubotuber pus, spider skins, and dragon dung. Try building some!

Magical Erumpent's horn contains fluid

Geode rock crystals have a glittery interior

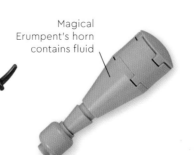

ANJELICA

EXPLODING FLUID

HALIWINKLES

DRAGON BONE MARROW

Bat and inverted
dome bottle stopper

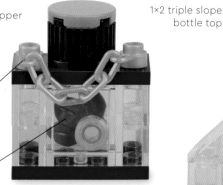

Small chain says
"keep away"

Leaf detail is
inside the bottle

1×2 triple slope
bottle top

POTENT POTIONS

Put something on each bottle to remind students of the contents while confusing nosy rivals. It could be a bat stopper for a flying potion, or a chain for a ghost-binding potion.

Opaque 1×2 brick
is a bottle label

Use different
colored plates
for a swirly potion

WHO'S TAKEN MY POTIONS BOOK?

SPECIAL PIECE

This 2×2 round plate with four vertical bars is often found on LEGO trees. Here, it connects the Bunsen burner tray to the stand.

Create unusual
ingredients to
heat up

4×4 radar dish
heating tray

Stand leg is a
swirly plant stem

BURNING AMBITION

A bunsen burner makes a small, very hot flame. It's ideal for cooking tiny ingredients, which are placed in a crucible above the burner.

Just three pieces
make a roaring
Bunsen burner

Flame attaches
to a plate
with clip

Pot is one
dome piece

SPIDERS

PLANGENTINES

Elongated bulb
is a balloon
bottom piece

PUNGOUS
ONION

DRAGON DUNG

HERBOLOGY LESSON

Professor Sprout is Head of Herbology at Hogwarts. She teaches students how to pick a perfect plum or muffle a Mandrake, but why stop there? Dig into your brick store and build some other magical plants, like Devil's Snare, Nux Myristica, or even a Venomous Tentacula, if you dare.

BUILD TIP

Don't overload your branches with too many Dirigible Plums, otherwise they'll be too heavy and the upward-growing fruit might hit the floor!

A PLUM JOB

Cultivate a crop of juicy Dirigible Plums on a greenhouse frame. When added to potions, these small, round, upward-growing fruits are said to enhance a person's ability to accept the extraordinary.

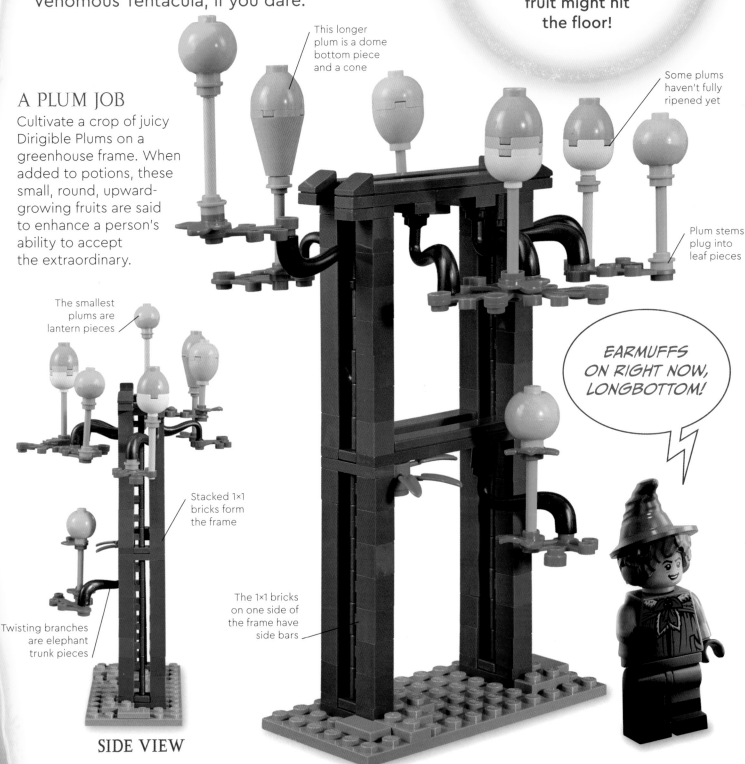

This longer plum is a dome bottom piece and a cone

Some plums haven't fully ripened yet

Plum stems plug into leaf pieces

The smallest plums are lantern pieces

Stacked 1×1 bricks form the frame

The 1×1 bricks on one side of the frame have side bars

Twisting branches are elephant trunk pieces

EARMUFFS ON RIGHT NOW, LONGBOTTOM!

SIDE VIEW

×1 round plates are crunched-up eyes

FRONT VIEW

CONNECTING ROOTS

The upper and lower roots attach to the Mandrake's body using different techniques so they can move in different ways. The top roots move up and down from that point, while the bottom ones move in and out.

1×2 plate with clip

1×2 plate with bar

1×2 hinge plate

The lower roots can move in three places

RESTORATIVE ROOTS

Mandrakes have human-shaped roots, which are used in many antidotes to curses and other magic spells. Fully grown Mandrakes give a fatal scream when unearthed, so wearing earmuffs is strongly recommended.

Dinosaur tail tip pieces hold the sprouting leaves

Palm tree leaf has a connecting clip

Open mouth, screaming loudly

A brown flower stem piece is perfect for roots

1×2 plates with bars and clips make the thickest parts of the root

This small horn fits into the side of a mechanical arm piece

Tan pieces highlight the rotund belly

SPECIAL PIECE

Parts of the twisted roots of the Mandrake are made from this long, curved horn piece, more often found on LEGO cattle. It has a small bar at the end.

WHERE DID I PUT THEM AGAIN?

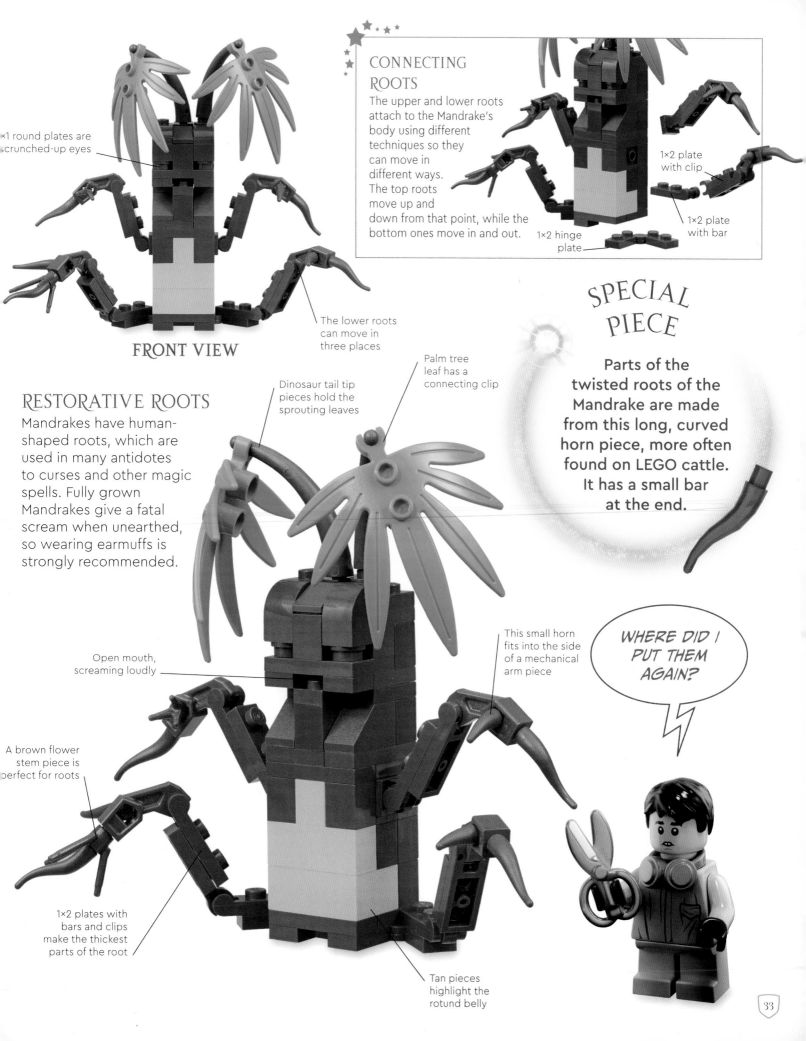

BOGGART CABINET

Create your own Defense Against the Dark Arts class with this Boggart build. Teacher Mad-Eye Moody gives your minifigures a tough lesson as they banish one Boggart, only to find another takes its place. The secret is in a sliding floor panel. What Boggart pair will you dream up from the darkest parts of your imagination?

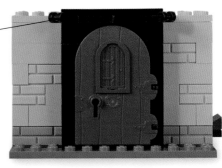

1×1 rounded plates with bars give the cabinet more shape

CLOSED VIEW

GHOST VIEW

SLIDE BY SLIDE

To banish a Boggart, students must use the "Riddikulus!" spell. Then shut the cabinet door, and slide the floor panel to the right. Did it disappear? Yes, but now a wailing Ghost Boggart has taken its place. Boo!

Creaky wooden door attaches to clips in the doorframe

RIDDIKULUS!

Boggart looms down from a one-brick-high platform

CABINET

6×12 base plate

SECRET SIDE
This rear view of the Boggart cabinet further reveals its secrets. The two-stud-wide sliding panel has a plate with rail along one side that passes through three bricks with grooves.

Secure your Boggarts on 2×2 jumper plates

Build another wall like this above the bricks with grooves

1×2 slope is a handle

1×8 plate with rail

Magnifying glass stand for examining strange finds

SPECIAL PIECE

This deceivingly clever 1×4 brick with groove has a horizontal gap along one of its sides. It's other long side looks like a regular 1×4 brick.

Stickered panels add an even creepier edge

Round brick and tile potion bottle

I KEEP A CLOSE EYE ON MY STUDENTS.

1×1 round brick cupboards

CLASSROOM

CORNISH PIXIE

Meet the Cornish pixie! This mini mischief maker squeals, throws books, and might even hang students up by the ears. Defense Against the Dark Arts Professor Gilderoy Lockhart couldn't control his pixies when he released them as a teaching aid, so don't bother using his Peskipiksi Pesternomi spell when it's time to banish your LEGO version to the brick box.

BUILD TIP

Build plenty of moving parts into your magical creatures to make them extra fun to play with. This pixie's arms, hands, legs, wings, head, and ears are all flexible.

The wrist moves on a clip and bar connection

Antenna is a 1x1 round plate with bar

1x1 cheese slope nose

Large, pointy ears shaped by curved and wedge slopes

Elbow joint is a hinge plate

1×1 round plate looks like a shrilly shouting mouth

Swirly cloud pieces for the wings

1×2 hinge plates for the knee

Ball joints and sockets let the thin arms swivel

Long, thin legs are narrow plates and tiles

1×2 plate with clip for the foot and a clawed toe

IMMOBULUS! THAT'S THE RIGHT SPELL.

LITTLE BLUE TERROR

Grab your brightest blue bricks to build this tiny troublemaker. Give it big, pointy ears and a pair of wings so it can fly. You could even try building a whole flock of these pixies. That really would spell trouble!

Legs can move at the hip and knee joints

FLUTTERING WINGS

Take a look at the back of the pixie's torso to figure out how the four parts of its wings connect. Black tiles with clips hold the wings. Those tiles attach to plates with clips that connect to rounded plates with bars on the body.

1×1 rounded plate with bar

1×1 tile with clip

2×2 plate secures the wing bases

DIVINATION CLASSROOM

Imagine what you'd see in Professor Trelawney's Divination classroom at Hogwarts and your future could hold some mystical LEGO models. Located high up in a tall tower, the circular classroom is decked out with sumptuous decor and filled with Divination materials that enable students to practice telling the future.

Border of red tiles makes a picture frame

Triangular tiles are the whites of an eye

Use lots of tiles for a smooth background

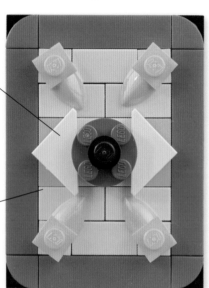

EYE

FLOWER

1×2 plate for a plant leaf

WHAT DO I SEE? ER... LOTS OF TEA!

Each picture has three layers of pieces

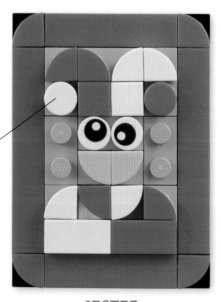

JESTER

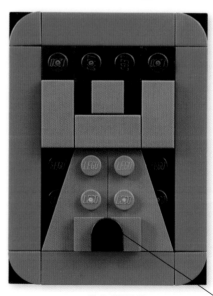

CASTLE

1×1 half circle tile is the castle door

STRANGE SYMBOLS

In Professor Trelawney's classroom, red drapes hang from the ceilings and symbolic artwork adorns the walls, creating a mysterious atmosphere. Design framed paintings bearing curious motifs to inspire (or confuse) Divination students.

BUILD TIP

The crystal ball is hollow so you can place round bricks, plates, or other small pieces inside it to suggest a fortune. If you don't have a ball, use a transparent dome.

CRYSTAL CLEAR

Ron can only see "a very foggy night" when he looks in his fortune-telling globe in the Divination classroom. What will your minifigures see when they stare into this LEGO crystal ball?

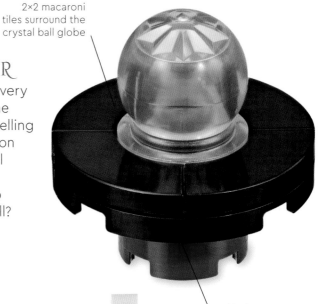

2×2 macaroni tiles surround the crystal ball globe

Table base is a 4×4 round plate

4×4 tan plate is milky tea dregs

1×2×1⅓ curved slope shapes the handle

Add a pattern or keep your cup plain

TEACUP

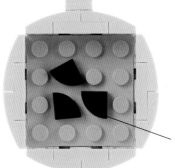

1×1 quarter tile black tea leaf

TOP VIEW

FORM IN A TEACUP

There are many empty teacups dotted around Professor Trelawney's classroom because she teaches the magical art of Tessomancy... reading the future in tea leaves. Build a cup, then attach dark pieces to resemble tea leaves.

UNDER THE LEAVES

Three sides of the teacup are built identically from plates and curved slopes, but the handle side of the cup incorporates a jumper plate and small slopes. All sides attach to hidden bricks with side studs inside the cup's base.

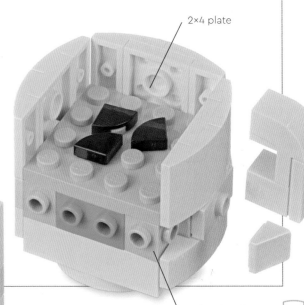

2×4 plate

TEASPOON

The bowl of the spoon is the back of 2×3 curved plate with hole

1×2 curved slope

1×1 brick with two side studs

SOUGHT-AFTER TREASURES

It's almost impossible to lay hands on the real Sorcerer's Stone. In the movies, it's sealed in a vault in Gringotts Bank. It's hard to get a peek at the Mirror of Erised, too. It's hidden somewhere inside Hogwarts. But there's nothing to stop you building your own LEGO versions of these mystical items. Secure them somewhere safe!

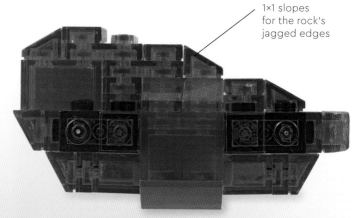

1×1 slopes for the rock's jagged edges

SIDE VIEW

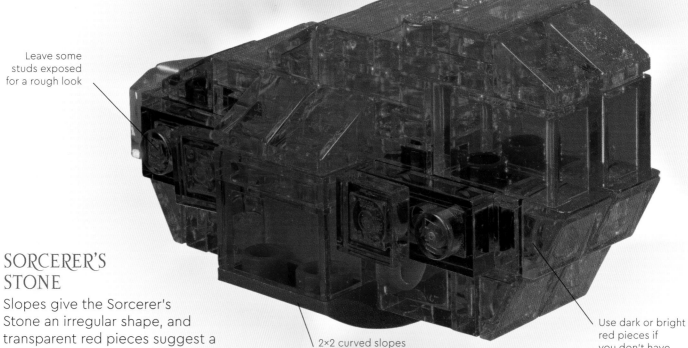

Leave some studs exposed for a rough look

2×2 curved slopes smooth out the stone's base

Use dark or bright red pieces if you don't have transparent ones

SORCERER'S STONE

Slopes give the Sorcerer's Stone an irregular shape, and transparent red pieces suggest a magical glow. What's the magic? The stone turns any metal into gold and can be used to create the Elixir of Life.

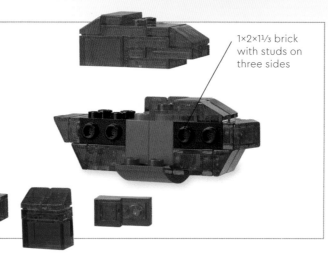

STUDDED CORE

The middle of the Sorcerer's Stone is built from opaque black and red bricks. The black bricks have side studs so you can attach transparent pieces sideways to them.

1×2×1⅓ brick with studs on three sides

I NEED THAT STONE!

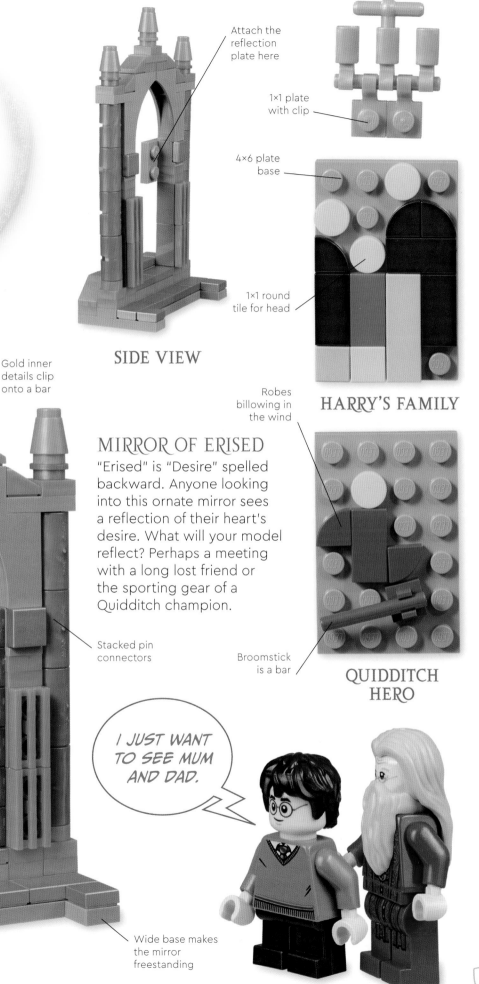

Attach the reflection plate here

1×1 plate with clip

4×6 plate base

1×1 round tile for head

SIDE VIEW

HARRY'S FAMILY

Mix tan and gold pieces for a painted wood look

Gold inner details clip onto a bar

Robes billowing in the wind

MIRROR OF ERISED

"Erised" is "Desire" spelled backward. Anyone looking into this ornate mirror sees a reflection of their heart's desire. What will your model reflect? Perhaps a meeting with a long lost friend or the sporting gear of a Quidditch champion.

Stacked pin connectors

Broomstick is a bar

QUIDDITCH HERO

I JUST WANT TO SEE MUM AND DAD.

Pearlescent blue tiles create a shimmering effect

Wide base makes the mirror freestanding

41

TOM RIDDLE'S DIARY

Why is Tom Riddle's diary blank? Well, it's waiting for someone to come and pour all their troubles into it. Tom (now Lord Voldemort) could use that kind of bad energy to strengthen his Dark powers. For a brighter book, build a diary for another student, a potion book, or even a yearbook for your favorite Hogwarts house.

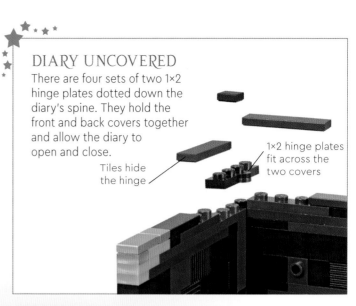

DIARY UNCOVERED
There are four sets of two 1×2 hinge plates dotted down the diary's spine. They hold the front and back covers together and allow the diary to open and close.

Tiles hide the hinge

1×2 hinge plates fit across the two covers

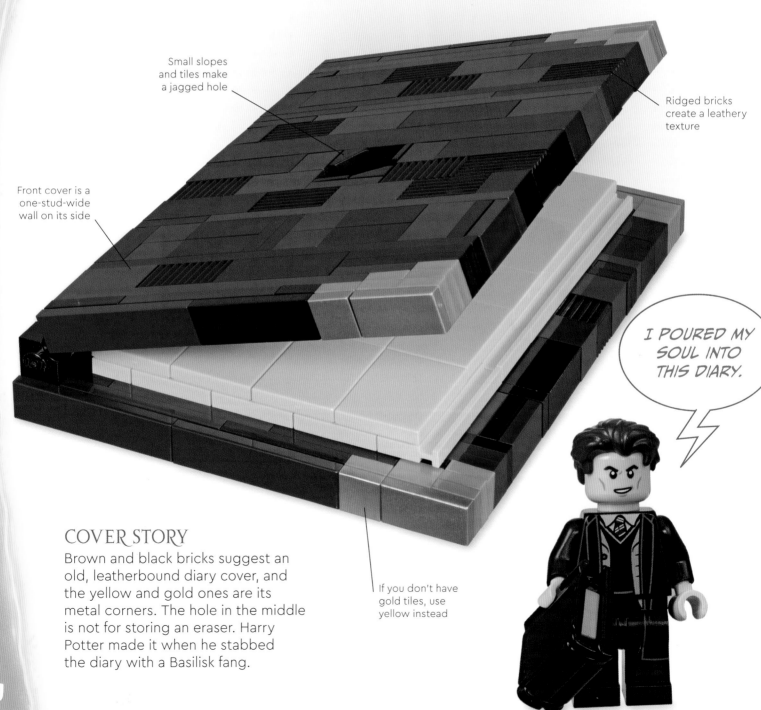

Small slopes and tiles make a jagged hole

Ridged bricks create a leathery texture

Front cover is a one-stud-wide wall on its side

I POURED MY SOUL INTO THIS DIARY.

COVER STORY
Brown and black bricks suggest an old, leatherbound diary cover, and the yellow and gold ones are its metal corners. The hole in the middle is not for storing an eraser. Harry Potter made it when he stabbed the diary with a Basilisk fang.

If you don't have gold tiles, use yellow instead

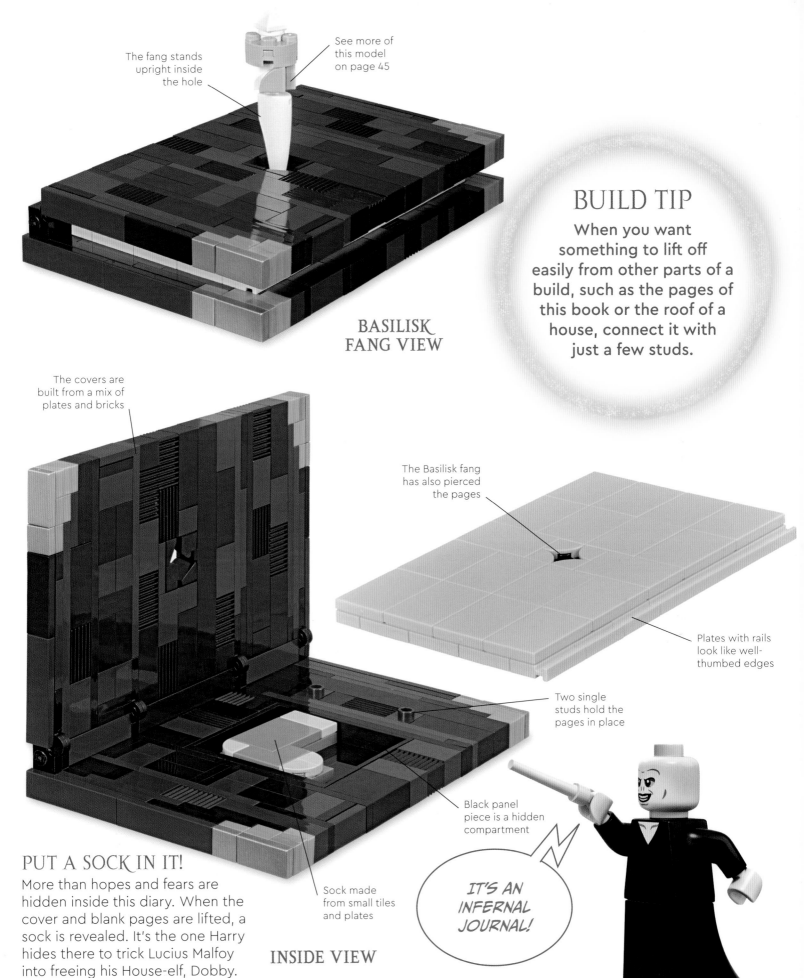

The fang stands upright inside the hole

See more of this model on page 45

BASILISK FANG VIEW

BUILD TIP
When you want something to lift off easily from other parts of a build, such as the pages of this book or the roof of a house, connect it with just a few studs.

The covers are built from a mix of plates and bricks

The Basilisk fang has also pierced the pages

Plates with rails look like well-thumbed edges

Two single studs hold the pages in place

Black panel piece is a hidden compartment

Sock made from small tiles and plates

PUT A SOCK IN IT!
More than hopes and fears are hidden inside this diary. When the cover and blank pages are lifted, a sock is revealed. It's the one Harry hides there to trick Lucius Malfoy into freeing his House-elf, Dobby.

INSIDE VIEW

IT'S AN INFERNAL JOURNAL!

POWERFUL POINTS

A witch or wizard needs to be pretty sharp to defeat a Dark Lord like Voldemort. Build a LEGO version of the mighty Sword of Gryffindor and fashion a Basilisk's tooth, and you'll have two of the sharpest objects in the wizarding world. Will they make the cut?

BUILD TIP

Include plates, slopes, and tiles in all different shapes and sizes to create an intricate, engraved look for the sword's precious metal hilt.

2×2 radar dish is an inset ruby

1×2 grille slopes attached sideways

Crossguard protects the wielder's fighting hand

The sword is made from pure silver, so use lots of gray pieces

Rubies symbolize the house of Gryffindor at Hogwarts

SHIELDING THE SWORD

The Sword has powerful magic, so Dumbledore has hidden it where only Gryffindor heroes can find it. Make your Sword suitably magnificent with a long, swishy blade and a ruby-encrusted hilt.

GRYFFINDOR HERO? YOU MUST HAVE THE WRONG NEVILLE!

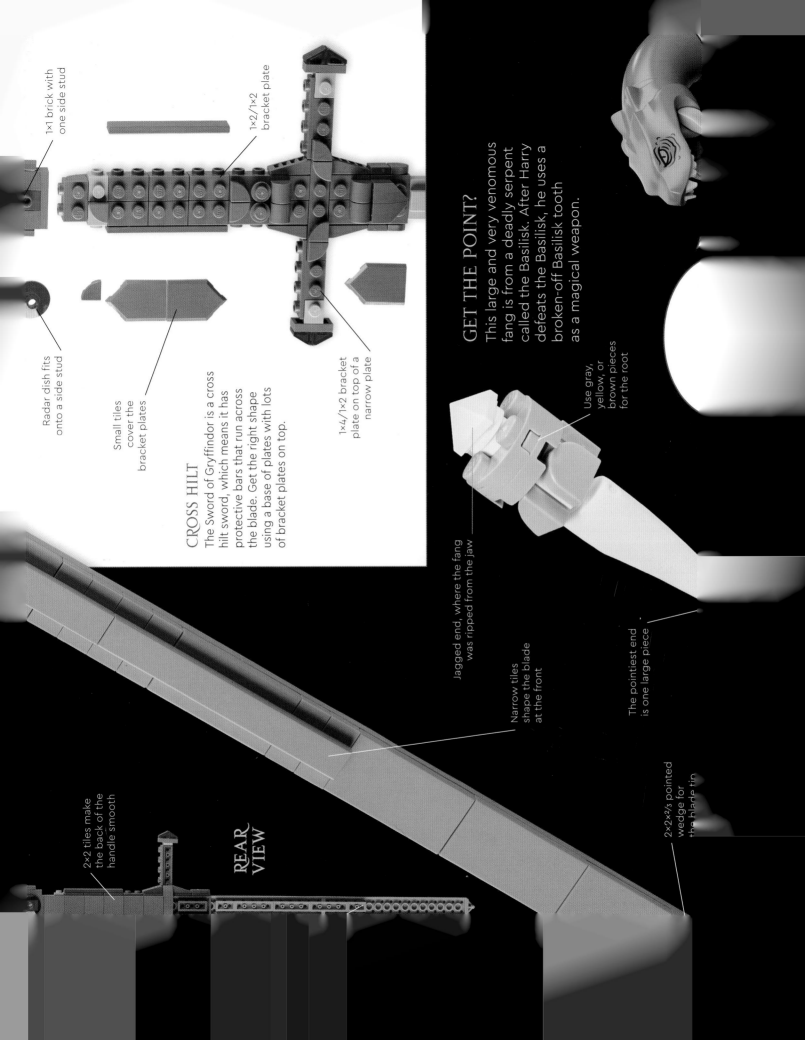

CROSS HILT

The Sword of Gryffindor is a cross hilt sword, which means it has protective bars that run across the blade. Get the right shape using a base of plates with lots of bracket plates on top.

1×1 brick with one side stud

1×2/1×2 bracket plate

Radar dish fits onto a side stud

Small tiles cover the bracket plates

1×4/1×2 bracket plate on top of a narrow plate

2×2 tiles make the back of the handle smooth

REAR VIEW

GET THE POINT?

This large and very venomous fang is from a deadly serpent called the Basilisk. After Harry defeats the Basilisk, he uses a broken-off Basilisk tooth as a magical weapon.

Use gray, yellow, or brown pieces for the root

Jagged end, where the fang was ripped from the jaw

Narrow tiles shape the blade at the front

The pointiest end is one large piece

2×2×⅔ pointed wedge for the blade tip

MARAUDER'S MAP

Who goes there? That's for you to decide. This three-dimensional Marauder's Map reveals the whereabouts of every minifigure in Hogwarts School and grounds. There are no hiding places here, even with an Invisibility Cloak! You could try making maps of other Harry Potter locations, like Hogsmeade Village or Malfoy Manor, too.

STORY MAP

Move minifigures or smaller microfigures around to create an unfolding adventure. Is that new student snooping around, or have they just got lost on their way to class? Your map can be as big and as detailed as you have space for.

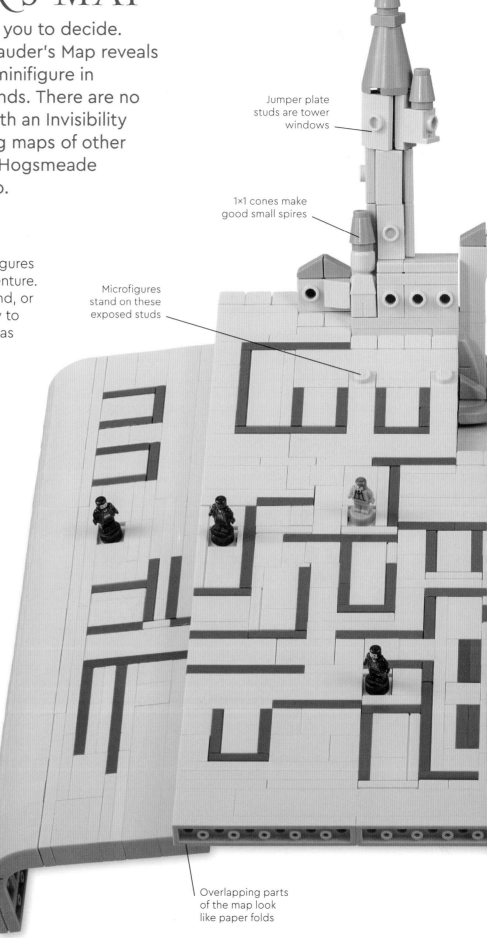

Jumper plate studs are tower windows

1×1 cones make good small spires

Microfigures stand on these exposed studs

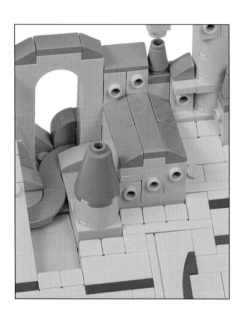

MEANDERING RIVER

A river curves through the rocky landscape that Hogwarts sits on. Fit two 2×2 macaroni tiles onto gray plates between your sloping rocks to get the same effect. Will your map also feature the Great Lake?

If you don't have lots of these arch pieces, you could make your map flat

Overlapping parts of the map look like paper folds

SPECIAL PIECE

The tiny figures on the Marauder's Map are called microfigures. They are just over one brick high, whereas LEGO minifigures are four bricks high.

Include a 1×4×2 arch for the viaduct

Hinge bricks and plates hold the castle upright

Build a strong base from bricks for a 3D map

The base slopes downward and the map rests on top

BACK VIEW

1×4 double curved slope forms a rounded corridor

LAYING DOWN PATHS

The pathways are built onto the map using sideways building techniques. Include bricks with studs on two sides to build sideways in two directions.

1×1 brick with two side studs

Tiles and plates make narrow paths

You could build Hogwarts landmarks as well as paths on your map

NEVILLE'S STUCK IN THE BATHROOM!

You could make your own tiny figures from small bricks or plates

WIZARD WHEEZES

If you like to laugh, create some of the hilarious wares from Weasleys' Wizard Wheezes in Diagon Alley. It's a joke shop run by Ron Weasley's twin brothers, Fred and George. It sells jokes galore, from dancing chickens to Portable Swamps. Go on, fill your boots with these bizarre builds (as long as they aren't Sticky Sneakers, or you might never leave the house!).

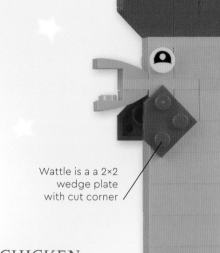

Wattle is a a 2×2 wedge plate with cut corner

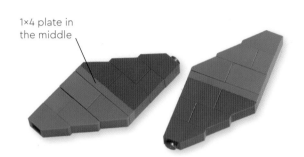

1×4 plate in the middle

Regular and slope bricks form each half

RUBBY O'CHICKEN

Who wouldn't want to own a bewitched rubber chicken? This one even does an Irish step dance. Get "clucking" your bricks together to build this fun feathered friend.

LEGO Technic pin connection

1×2 curved slopes shape each foot

PUKING PASTILLES

These candies can help Hogwarts students get out of classes. If they eat the green half, they throw up. Once they're excused, they eat the purple half and yay... instant recovery! Just don't eat these LEGO versions, or you'll be excused for a trip to the dentist!

STEP UP! STEP UP! JOKES FOR ALL!

BUILD TIP

Give your chicken two movable legs to jig with. The legs on the build above connect with LEGO Technic pins, which allow the legs to swing from side to side.

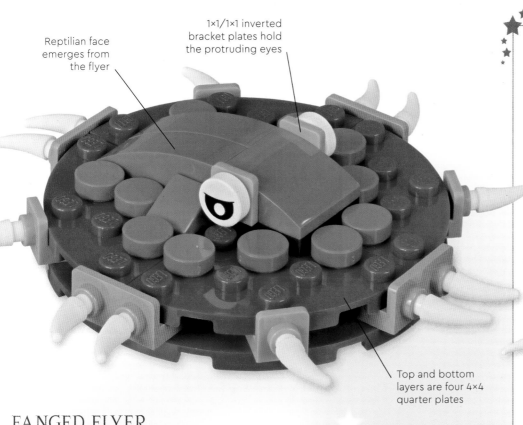

Reptilian face emerges from the flyer

1×1/1×1 inverted bracket plates hold the protruding eyes

FANG SANDWICH
The fanged flyer is built in three layers. Lurking beneath the top and bottom layers are inverted bracket plates, which hold the fangs, and a round plate that makes the flyer more stable.

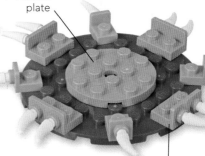

4×4 round plate

1×2/1×2 inverted bracket plate

Top and bottom layers are four 4×4 quarter plates

FANGED FLYER
This spinning disk is built for whizzing through the air. But watch your fingers when you use it—it's got sharp teeth all around the edge. Perhaps you could build a protective Handler's Glove, too.

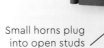

Small horns plug into open studs

SIDE VIEW

LEGO hose is the extendable string

Curved slopes form the ear's outer rim

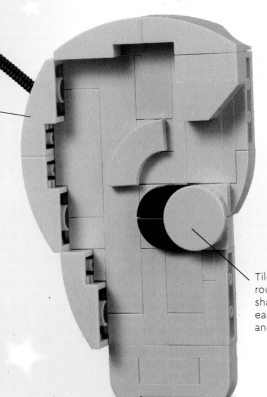

EXTENDABLE EAR
This listening device is ideal for eavesdropping on someone discreetly. Just make sure there are no cats nearby first. They may mistake the ear part for a piece of bacon, like Hermione's cat Crookshanks once did!

Tiles with rounded shapes create ear curves and folds

REAR VIEW

THE WEASLEYS' KITCHEN ITEMS

Cook up some LEGO magic for the Weasleys' kitchen at The Burrow. With a large family like theirs, things could easily descend into chaos for Molly and Arthur Weasley. Luckily, Ron's mom has organizational skills that are second to none... and a selection of marvelously magical ways to get some help around the house.

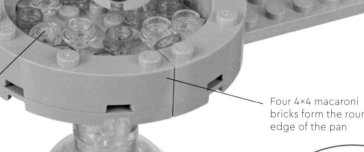

Two stacked 1×1 round plates let the brush "float"

SIDE VIEW

WIZARDLY WASHING UP

At The Burrow, the Weasley family can sit down and relax after a meal. The dishes? They take care of themselves. The pan hovers over the sink while an enchanted brush scrubs the grease away.

Brush handle is a telescope piece

1×1 round plates for soap suds

Four 4×4 macaroni bricks form the round edge of the pan

The pan hovers on transparent round bricks

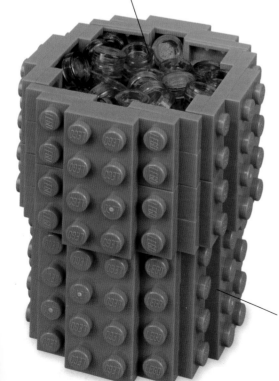

Green floo powder crystals are 1×1 round tiles

Layers of plates attach sideways to make the pot

CATCH THE FLOO

By the kitchen fireplace there's a pot of Floo Powder. In the movies, the Weasleys use this glittery dust to travel via the Floo Network. They just grab a handful, stand in the fireplace, state their destination, and...

LET'S CREATE SELF-MAKING TEA NEXT.

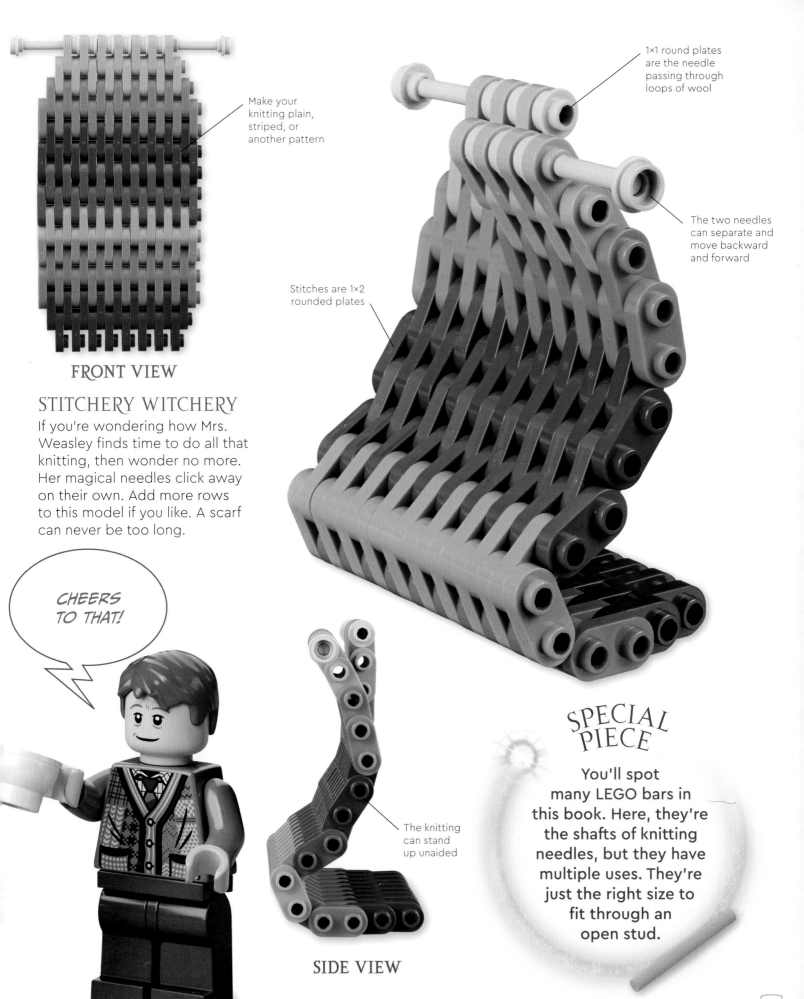

FRONT VIEW

Make your knitting plain, striped, or another pattern

1×1 round plates are the needle passing through loops of wool

The two needles can separate and move backward and forward

Stitches are 1×2 rounded plates

STITCHERY WITCHERY

If you're wondering how Mrs. Weasley finds time to do all that knitting, then wonder no more. Her magical needles click away on their own. Add more rows to this model if you like. A scarf can never be too long.

CHEERS TO THAT!

The knitting can stand up unaided

SIDE VIEW

SPECIAL PIECE

You'll spot many LEGO bars in this book. Here, they're the shafts of knitting needles, but they have multiple uses. They're just the right size to fit through an open stud.

TIME-TRAVELING DEVICES

Imagine being able to turn back time by a few hours, or store all your memories somewhere for future use. You'd never miss a bus again... or forget why on Earth you chose that unflattering robe. That's what both the Time-Turner and the Pensieve can do in the wizarding world. Start building these magical items, and time will surely fly.

Link lots of LEGO chains for a long necklace

Gold bar piece connects the chain to the pendant

Inverted slope bricks make a rounded hole

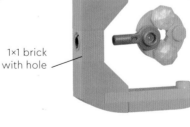

LEGO Technic half pin

1×1 round plate with bar

1×1 brick with hole

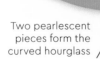

Two pearlescent pieces form the curved hourglass

Hourglass, mid-turn

SIDE VIEW

TIME-TURNER

A Time-Turner is a pendant that has the shape of a tiny hourglass at its center. Hermione borrowed one from Professor McGonagall so she could turn back time and fit extra classes into her timetable. Build yours with a spinning middle section.

IN A SPIN

The center of the Time-Turner spins via half pins plugged into holes. Gold 1×1 round plates with bars connect the pins to the 2×2 round plate that holds the hourglass shape, allowing it to spin freely.

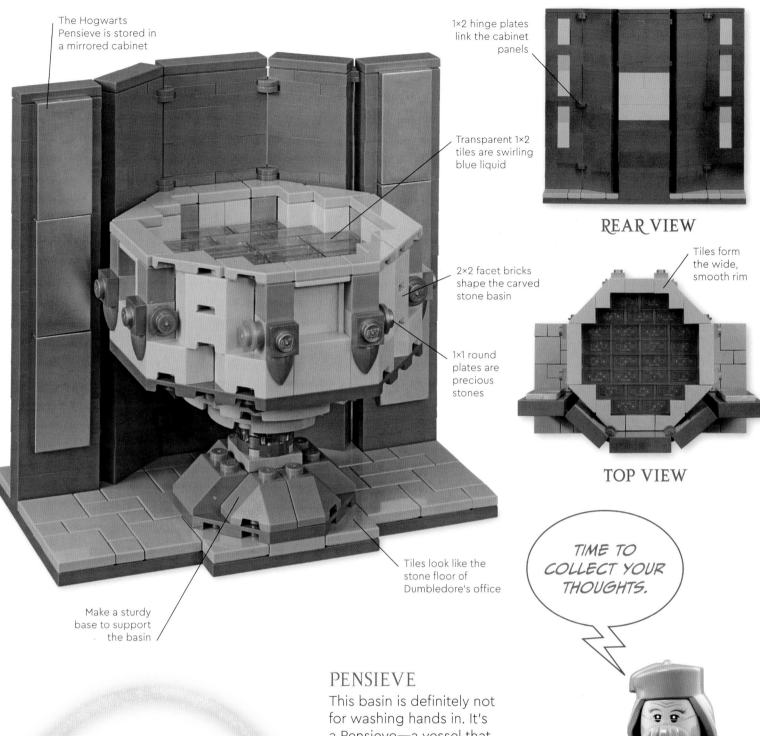

The Hogwarts Pensieve is stored in a mirrored cabinet

1×2 hinge plates link the cabinet panels

Transparent 1×2 tiles are swirling blue liquid

REAR VIEW

2×2 facet bricks shape the carved stone basin

1×1 round plates are precious stones

Tiles form the wide, smooth rim

TOP VIEW

Tiles look like the stone floor of Dumbledore's office

Make a sturdy base to support the basin

BUILD TIP

Adorn your mystical pensieve with precious stones and strange symbols. Build bricks with side studs into your basin so you can attach extra pieces.

PENSIEVE

This basin is definitely not for washing hands in. It's a Pensieve—a vessel that holds the memories of a witch or wizard. Magical folk leave their thoughts in Pensieves to look back on in future days.

TIME TO COLLECT YOUR THOUGHTS.

This metal dish is a small Pensieve

ANIMAGUS

An Animagus is a wizard or witch who can transform into an animal. It's a furry useful disguise! Why not choose an animal and build a LEGO Animagus for yourself? Pick a creature that represents your style and personality. Perhaps it could be wearing your favorite item of clothing or resemble you in another way.

SPECIAL PIECE

This 1×1 rounded plate with bar is a versatile piece. Not only can it move when its bar is connected to a clip—it can also make a convincing animal paw.

CAT'S EYES

If a Hogwarts student is late to Professor McGonagall's classroom, they should not presume they've got away with it just because they can't see her. This silver tabby cat is her Animagus, and she could be watching their every move.

Include black plates for tabby stripes

Exposed studs look like longer fur

4×4 round plate for the hat brim

Whiskers are minifigure claw weapons

1×2 jumper plate centers the nose

REAR VIEW

Tail curves around thanks to two ball and socket connections

YOU'RE TOP DOG, SIRIUS.

1×1 round brick front legs

FACE OFF

The cat's face and chest curves connect to its body using sideways building. The facial features all connect to one 2×3 plate. That plate attaches to two inbuilt 1×1 bricks with side studs.

2×3 plate is the face base

1×2×1⅓ brick with four side studs

2×2 curved slope

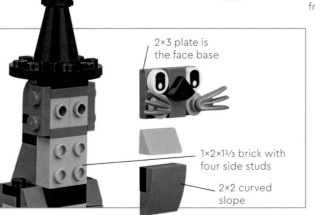

Mix in gray pieces to illuminate the black fur

The tail is flexible in three places

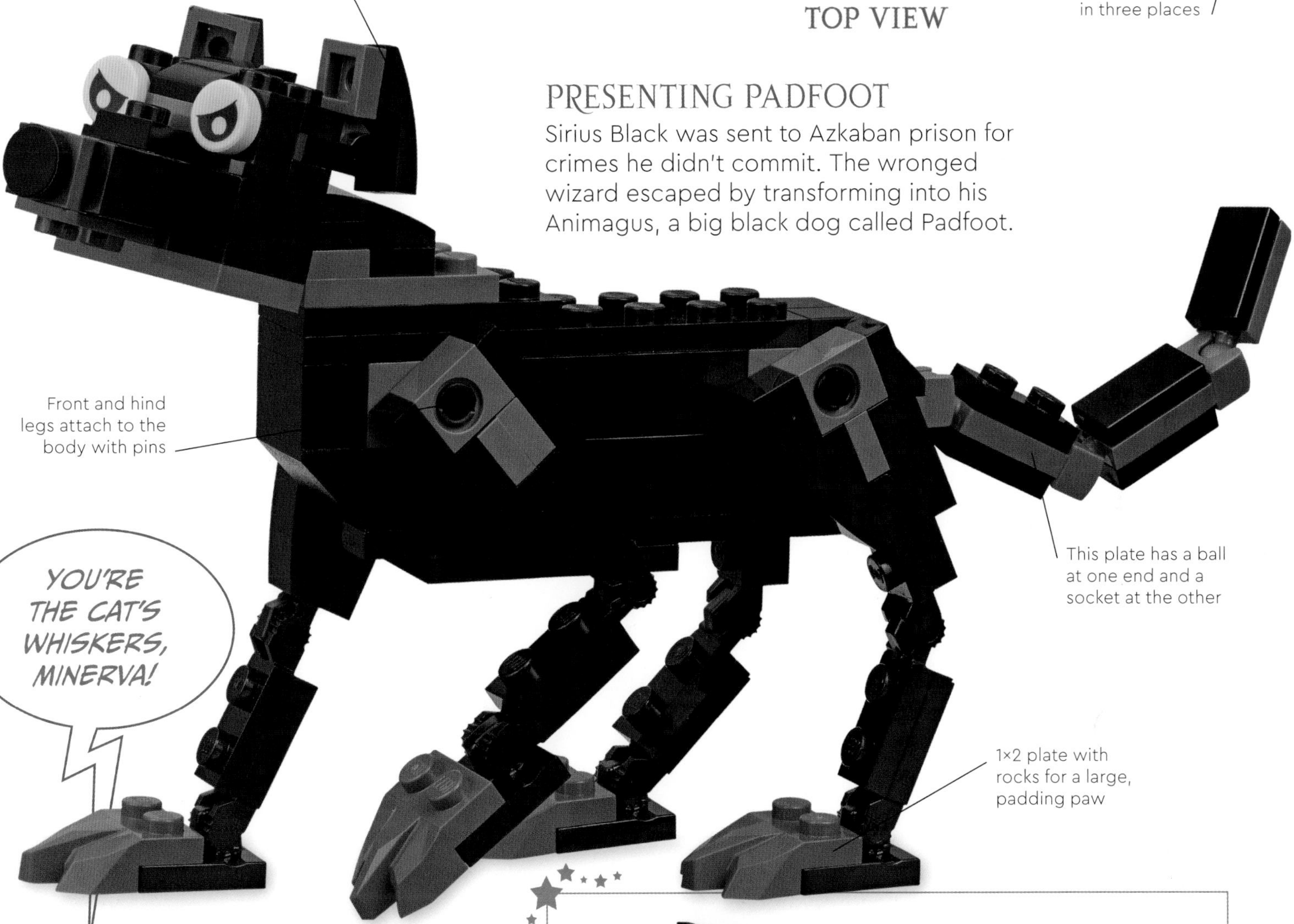

Ears are 1×2 curved slopes and plates with clips

PRESENTING PADFOOT

Sirius Black was sent to Azkaban prison for crimes he didn't commit. The wronged wizard escaped by transforming into his Animagus, a big black dog called Padfoot.

Front and hind legs attach to the body with pins

This plate has a ball at one end and a socket at the other

YOU'RE THE CAT'S WHISKERS, MINERVA!

1×2 plate with rocks for a large, padding paw

Narrowed eye tile

1×2 tile

1×1 round tile nose

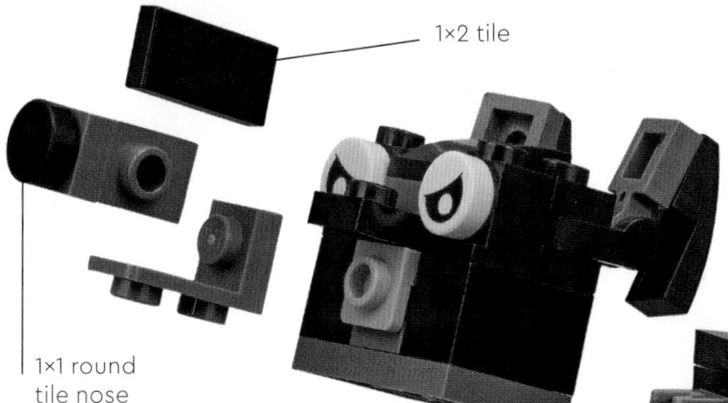

SNOUTING ABOUT

Padfoot's sizable snout is built around a 1×1 brick with studs on opposite sides. Two 1×2 tiles cover the exposed studs for a smooth finish.

FRONT VIEW

55

COMPETITIVE CUPS

Eyes on the prize! Build a gleaming cup for the winner of the Triwizard Tournament—a dangerous contest between Hogwarts and two other famous schools of magic. You'll need a Goblet of Fire, too, to hold and choose the names of the courageous entrants. What other magical Harry Potter-themed trophies or goblets could you build with your LEGO elements?

SPECIAL PIECE

This marbled, glitter-flecked flame piece has a bar at one end so it can plug into an open stud. You could also use it as a wave of water or a wondrous wing.

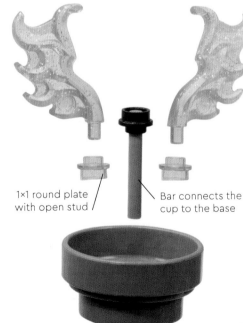

HOTLY CONTESTED

Entrants write their names on paper and drop them into the Goblet of Fire. After 24 hours, its flames churn out a (slightly charred) champion to represent each school. Nobody under 17 can enter—a magical barrier keeps away anyone younger.

Blue flames cross over for a roaring fire effect

IS THERE AN UPPER AGE LIMIT?

1×1 plates with clips are carved details

1×1 brick with two side studs

Round bricks and plates form the long stem

FIRE IT UP

The cup part of the Goblet of Fire is a special 4×4 round brick, which has seven holes inside. The flame pieces fit into the holes via 1×1 round plates with open studs.

1×1 round plate with open stud

Bar connects the cup to the base

2×2 round tile with hole

Two 4×4 round plates

GLITTERING TROPHY

This cup has elements that look like glass and metal. If you like, you could add magical-looking elements to yours, like reptile-shaped handles. Will Harry raise it aloft for Hogwarts, or will victory go to Beauxbatons' Academy of Magic or Durmstrang Institute?

Handles don't attach to the top of the cup

Four 2×2 macaroni tiles make a circular rim

Transparent blue pieces look like glowing glass

Include a 4×4 radar dish for a curved base

Stacked 2×2 round bricks and plates

2×2 macaroni tiles give the base a smooth finish

Two 4×4 round plates sit below the rim

TOP VIEW

SIMPLE HANDLES

The curved handles of this cup are each made from just three pieces. They clip onto a 2×2 round plate with octagonal bar.

1×2×1⅓ curved slope

2×2 plate with octagonal bar

1×2 plate with clip

I'LL CHALLENGE ANYONE FOR THAT CUP!

TRI WIZ ARD

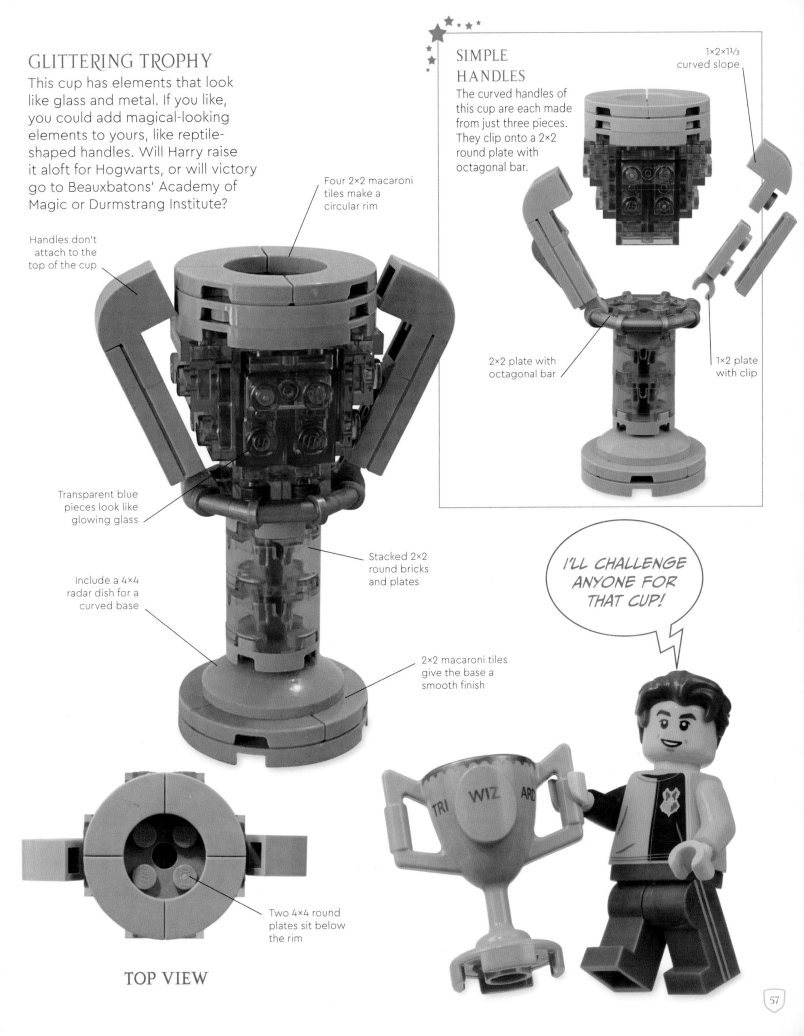

MAGIC BAG

A witch or wizard on the go needs something to carry their wand, spell book, and other magical gear around in. But why have a regular bag when you can have an enchanted one, like Hermione's beaded pouch? Give building it a try and you may just get carried away.

BUILD TIP

The drawstring top of the bag is built around a 2×2 round plate with octagonal bar. Eight small curved sections can clip onto its eight bars.

ONE BAG FULL

Hermione's small, purple-striped handbag looks barely big enough to hold a chocolate frog. Yet she has been known to stow various changes of clothes, the Sword of Gryffindor, and even a camping tent inside it. That's magic!

1×2 curved slopes and plates with clips form each of these sections

1×3 curved slopes are gathered material

NOW WHERE DID I PUT MY KEYS?

1×4 curved slopes look like striped embroidered cloth

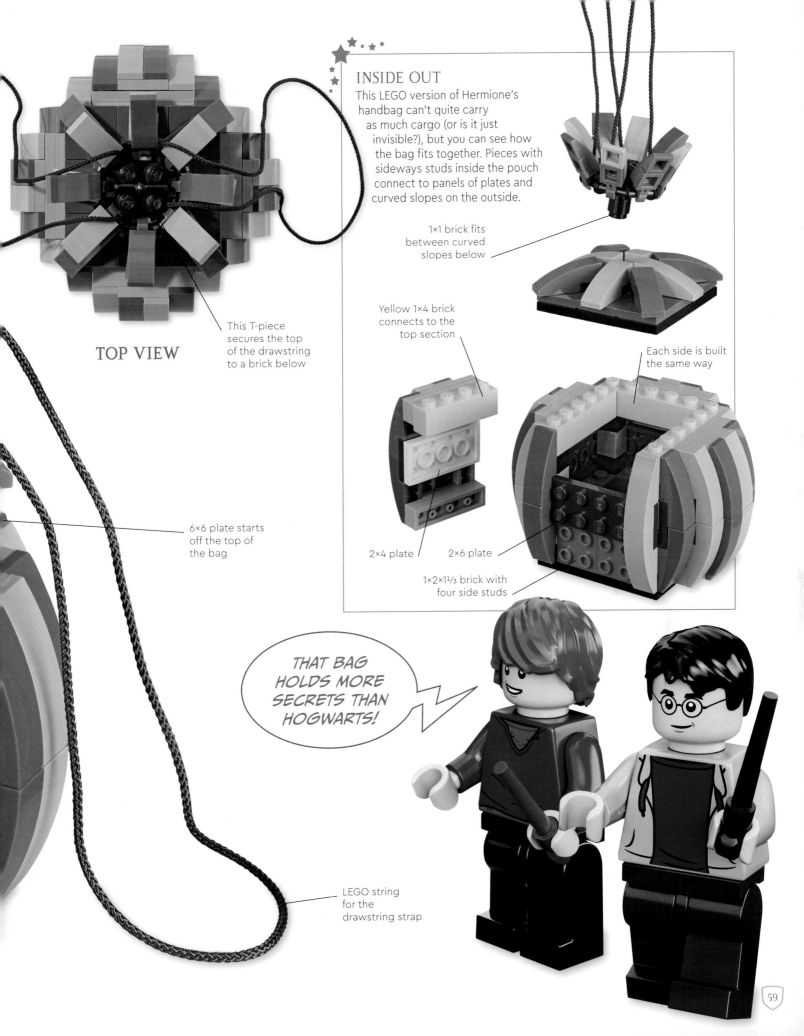

TOP VIEW

This T-piece secures the top of the drawstring to a brick below

INSIDE OUT

This LEGO version of Hermione's handbag can't quite carry as much cargo (or is it just invisible?), but you can see how the bag fits together. Pieces with sideways studs inside the pouch connect to panels of plates and curved slopes on the outside.

1×1 brick fits between curved slopes below

Yellow 1×4 brick connects to the top section

Each side is built the same way

6×6 plate starts off the top of the bag

2×4 plate

2×6 plate

1×2×1⅓ brick with four side studs

THAT BAG HOLDS MORE SECRETS THAN HOGWARTS!

LEGO string for the drawstring strap

59

BUTTERBEERS ALL AROUND

Mmmmm... Butterbeer! This butterscotch-flavored beverage certainly tastes magical. Many wizarding folk visit the Hog's Head or the Three Broomsticks to pick some up, but you can build a barrel and glass from LEGO bricks and serve your Harry Potter minifigures in your own home.

GREAT SIZE!

Glass base is a 4×4 round plate with hole

SIDE VIEW

Some of the foam is dripping over the edge

HOT OR COLD?

Butterbeer can be drunk cold on a hot day or hot on a cold day. When heated, it forms a sweet, foaming head on the top of a glass or tankard.

2×2 domes are large foam bubbles

TOP VIEW

Transparent tankard handle

This yellow plate could be a ring of Butterbeer under the glass

BELOW THE FOAM

Peek beneath the foaming head of the Butterbeer to see how the tankard is built. Its sides are shaped by 1×4 double curved slopes that attach to bricks with side studs.

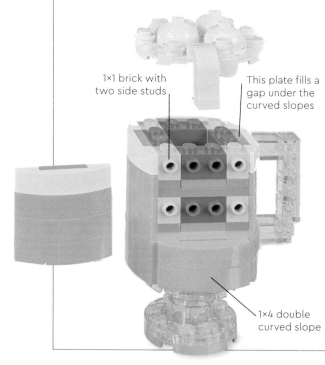

1×1 brick with two side studs

This plate fills a gap under the curved slopes

1×4 double curved slope

Black tiles look like a hoop around the barrel

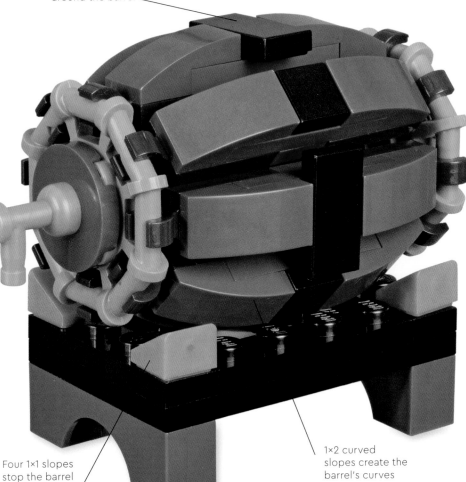

The 2×2 round plate with octagonal bar is particularly useful for building circular models, from a barrel like this to an octopus's body or a spaceship.

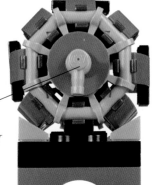

ROLL OUT THE BARREL

Slowly does it! Butterbeer takes time to sweeten. A few months in a wooden barrel inside an old, stone cellar does the job. Why not build racks filled with other beverage bottles for a complete cellar scene?

Dispensing tap attaches to a 2×2 round jumper plate

FRONT VIEW

Four 1×1 slopes stop the barrel from rolling

1×2 curved slopes create the barrel's curves

Arch bricks for the stand's legs

PERFECT WITH A PUMPKIN PASTY!

BARREL BUILD

The middle of this Butterbeer barrel build is hollow. There is a round plate with octagonal bar at either end of it, and eight separate side panels. Two plates with clips on each side panel hold the two round plates together.

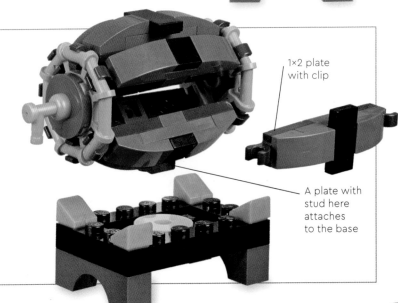

1×2 plate with clip

A plate with stud here attaches to the base

61

WANTED POSTER

Do you recognize the wizard on this wanted poster? It's Sirius Black, on the run after breaking out of Azkaban prison. Sirius was convicted of killing Muggles, but he says he's innocent. Will anyone turn Sirius in to the Dementors pursuing him? There's a reward of 5,000 Galleons.

HAVE YOU SEEN HIM?

The Sirius on the poster looks like he's seen you, too. Try adding some moving features, such as the eyebrows or mouth, to convey the prisoner's desperate efforts to communicate his innocence.

The picture is five plates wide in places

SPECIAL PIECE

The humble 1×1 quarter tile is a useful piece for creating letters, numbers, and patterns with curves. It can also add texture to your builds.

2×2 wedge plates serve as wild, overgrown hair

SIDE VIEW

Narrow tiles make a black frame

BASE VIEW

Poster is built on one 16×16 base plate

Two half circle
tiles for each
expressive
eyebrow

Staring eyes are 2×2
round jumper plates
and 1×1 round tiles

HELP! I'VE
BEEN FRAMED.

Sirius holds a board
bearing symbols and
his prisoner number

Fingers are
curved slopes
and tiles

CHAPTER TWO

MOVIE MOMENTS

Every Harry Potter movie is jam-packed with unforgettable moments. Who could forget meandering down Diagon Alley, boarding the Hogwarts Express, or Harry and Ron's narrow escape in the Forbidden Forest? Re-create some of those moments in LEGO® form with this super selection of iconic scenes.

PRIVET DRIVE

This tidy residence is home to the Dursleys: Harry's aunt, uncle, and cousin. They're proud Muggles, so shhh... don't tell the neighbors there's a wizard in the family! Cousin Dudley is stomping around upstairs, but where's Harry? Find him in his bedroom—the cramped, dark cupboard under the stairs.

UNWELCOME MAIL
Leave a small gap in the back of the fireplace for letter-printed tiles to whoosh through, whether the Dursleys like it or not.

Striped wallpaper is stacked 1×1 bricks

Tile curtains attach sideways

GRRR, POTTER!

TV screen is a transparent 1×2 tile

The four-piece suite matches the wallpaper

Add Dursley details, like cookies on the coffee table

Purple base plate is a plush carpet

SITTING ROOM
Use "tasteful" tones for this sitting room build, and build matching furniture and a mantlepiece topped with Muggle ornaments. Be warned: the Dursleys don't like any letters from Hogwarts or mischievous House-elves in their house. How much magical mayhem can you create?

Cake appears to float on transparent pieces

LEVITATING CAKE

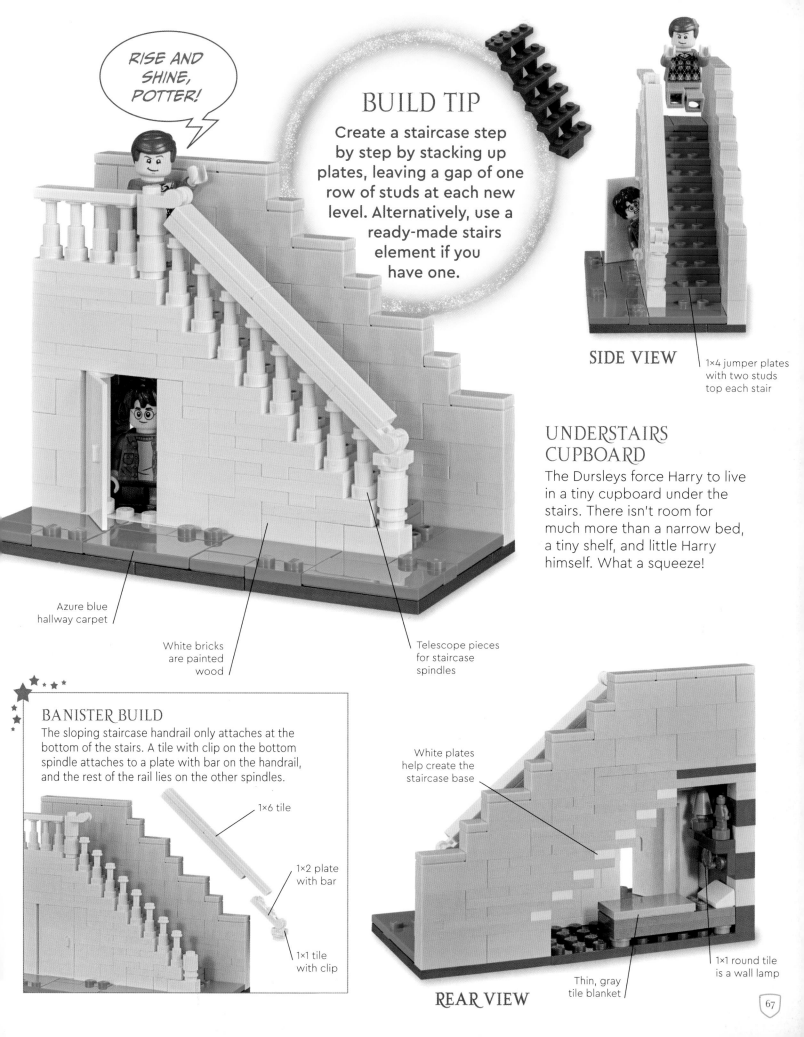

RISE AND SHINE, POTTER!

BUILD TIP

Create a staircase step by step by stacking up plates, leaving a gap of one row of studs at each new level. Alternatively, use a ready-made stairs element if you have one.

SIDE VIEW

1×4 jumper plates with two studs top each stair

UNDERSTAIRS CUPBOARD

The Dursleys force Harry to live in a tiny cupboard under the stairs. There isn't room for much more than a narrow bed, a tiny shelf, and little Harry himself. What a squeeze!

Azure blue hallway carpet

White bricks are painted wood

Telescope pieces for staircase spindles

BANISTER BUILD

The sloping staircase handrail only attaches at the bottom of the stairs. A tile with clip on the bottom spindle attaches to a plate with bar on the handrail, and the rest of the rail lies on the other spindles.

1×6 tile

1×2 plate with bar

1×1 tile with clip

White plates help create the staircase base

1×1 round tile is a wall lamp

Thin, gray tile blanket

REAR VIEW

HARRY'S BEDROOM

When he's back home on Privet Drive, Harry tends to stay upstairs in his room. Well, you might, too, if you knew his relatives, the Dursleys! This build shows Harry's bedroom, complete with his bed, desk, and Gryffindor flag to remind him of Hogwarts. The cabinet in the corner could contain clothes, linens, or even a (sometimes) helpful House-elf.

FRONT VIEW

BOX ROOM

Harry's bedroom might be the smallest one in the Dursley residence, but it's far better than the cupboard under the stairs where he used to live. There's room for a wider bed and furniture.

Lamp for secretly studying spells by

Curved slopes and tiles form the Gryffindor flag

2×2 wedge plates for tied-back curtains

BAD DOBBY!

Lampshade is a 2×2 truncated cone

Stool made from four 1×1 cones and a 2×2 plate

Plates are a soft rug on the wooden floor

BEDROOM BASE

Learn to build a basic room base and you'll be able to create all kinds of living spaces for your minifigures. Add two brick-built walls to a base plate, planning where you want wall and floor furniture by leaving exposed studs to attach them to.

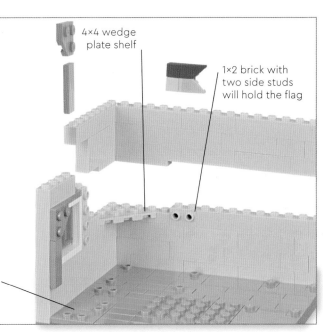

4×4 wedge plate shelf

1×2 brick with two side studs will hold the flag

The end of the desk will fit onto this jumper plate

THIS IS NOT A GOOD TIME FOR A HOUSE-ELF VISIT!

Deep cabinet for hiding House-elves

Narrow tiles are hard floorboards

1×1 slopes for tucked-in bed covers

BED

Desktop has studs on one side

1×2 jumper plate drawers

DESK AND STOOL

1×4×6 door piece is built into brick cabinet sides

CABINET

HUT ON THE ROCKS

Imagine being stuck in a drafty hut on a rock out at sea! That's where Harry's mean Uncle Vernon takes him, hoping to keep the young wizard away from Hogwarts. The bed is lumpy and the sofa stinks of seaweed. Poor, damp Harry! Will you send Hagrid to rescue him?

Small windows are less likely to be broken in a storm

NO ONE WILL FIND US HERE... OH!

Ingot pieces attached sideways stick out from the rest of the brickwork

BUILD TIP

The exterior brickwork of the hut on the rocks looks sea-beaten and uneven because it's built from a mixture of regular, textured, and round pieces.

Olive green pieces are moss-covered bricks

YOU'RE ON THE FLOOR, POTTER!

Transparent pieces are waves crashing against the rocks

RICKETY RESIDENCE

Leave the back of the hut open so you can move Harry and his visitors between the two stories. Will it be upstairs, where salty wind whistles through the window? Or downstairs, where choppy seawater soaks through the furniture?

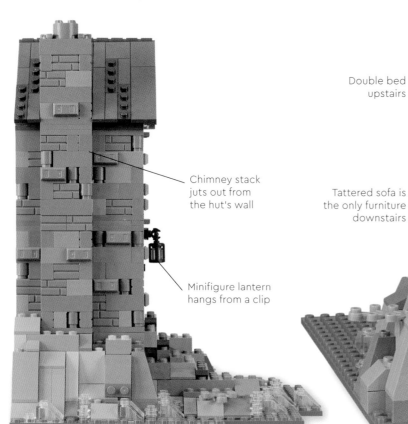

2×2 round brick chimney pot

Exposed studs look like roof damage

Double bed upstairs

Tattered sofa is the only furniture downstairs

Small fire warms the hut

Chimney stack juts out from the hut's wall

Minifigure lantern hangs from a clip

Add more rocks here or keep it flat like this

SIDE VIEW

REAR VIEW

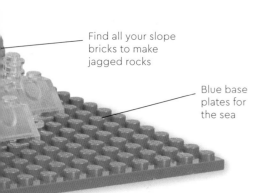

Find all your slope bricks to make jagged rocks

Blue base plates for the sea

WEATHERED ROOF

Each side of the sloping wooden roof is built from narrow plates and tiles on the top, with larger plates underneath. Hinge bricks and plates on the rafters allow them to fit onto the hut diagonally.

Row of 1×1 round bricks rests on the rooftop

Leave a gap for the chimney

1×2 hinge brick and 2×2 hinge plate

THE LEAKY CAULDRON

Your minifigures can enjoy a Butterbeer with Harry at the Leaky Cauldron, London's oldest and most magical inn. This build shows the downstairs area, where weary wizards and witches share drinks, snacks, and gossip. It's a nice place to take the weight off your broomstick for half an hour!

Old-fashioned lattice windows ensure patrons' privacy

CONVIVIAL VIBE

Long tables create a sociable atmosphere at this inn on Diagon Alley. It's the perfect venue to gather over a meal or refreshing beverage. Your minifigures can find a spot by the fire, dust off a stool, and join the magical gang. Pets welcome!

I CAN'T TELL YOU HOW PLEASED I AM TO MEET YOU.

Plastered walls are crumbling in places

Newspapers and tankards litter the tables

2×2 tiles are flagstones in the uneven floor

BUBBLING CAULDRON

The contents of this cauldron are up to you—will it be filled with Butterbeer; exploding lemonade; or the house special, Leaky Soup? Build a large hearth with logs, a roaring fire, and metal grates to rest your cauldron on.

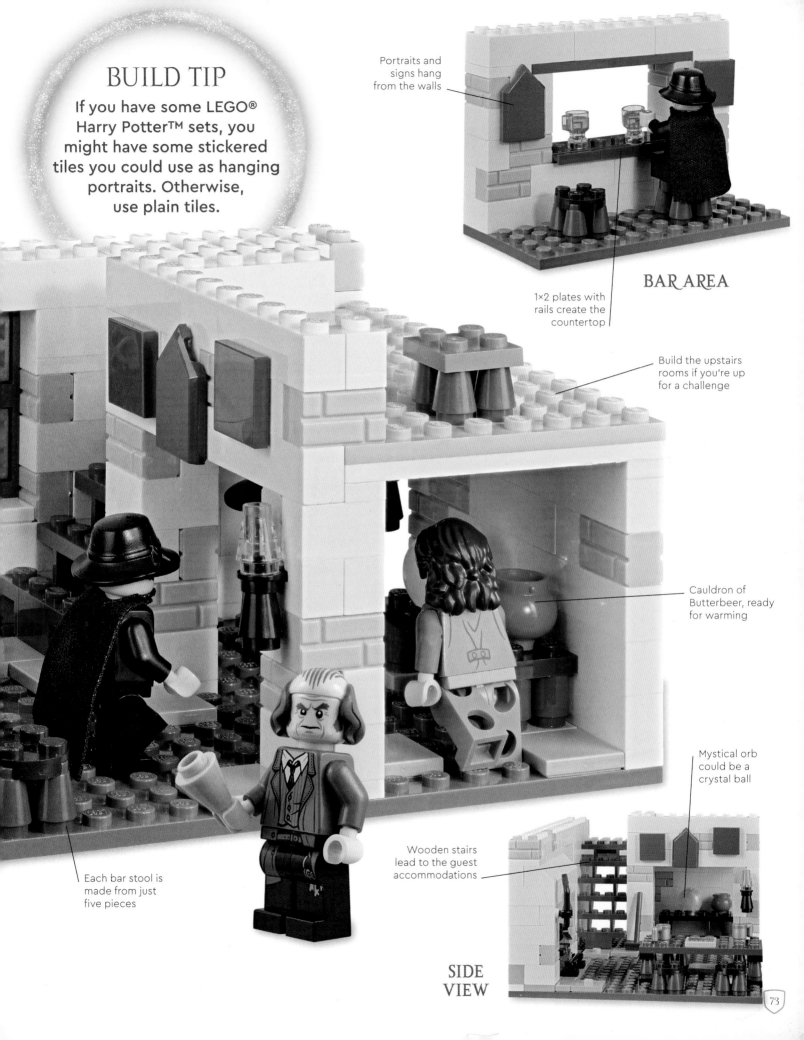

Portraits and
signs hang
from the walls

1×2 plates with
rails create the
countertop

BAR AREA

Build the upstairs
rooms if you're up
for a challenge

Cauldron of
Butterbeer, ready
for warming

Mystical orb
could be a
crystal ball

Wooden stairs
lead to the guest
accommodations

Each bar stool is
made from just
five pieces

**SIDE
VIEW**

73

BORGIN & BURKES

If a wizard or witch ever finds themselves lost in Knockturn Alley, they should under no circumstances enter Borgin & Burkes to ask for help. This dusty antique shop is filled with... things. Unpleasant things. Build a model of the grimy shop front to hint at the strange wares within. And then perhaps step away...

Slope bricks add a hint of a tile roof

Drainpipe is stacked candle accessories

1×1 round plates in the walls look like crumbling brickwork

A DARK PLACE

The outside of the shop as well as the inside is dark. Maybe that's because Borgin & Burkes is known to attract customers who practice... whisper it... the Dark Arts. Do you dare to look through the windows?

Plates with clips hold the drainpipe in place

Tile sign hangs from a 1×2 plate with two clips

SIDE VIEW

THERE WON'T BE ANY MUGGLES IN HERE.

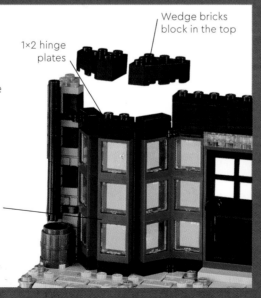

BAY BRICKS

The enticing bay windows of Borgin & Burkes are made in separate panels. Three of the panels curve outward and connect at the top and bottom with hinge plates.

1×2 hinge plates

Wedge bricks block in the top

Stacked 2×2 window panels

Leave exposed studs for an uneven cobbled street

The attic windows are small

REAR VIEW

What will you build to display in the windows?

IS MALFOY GOING INTO THAT SHOP?

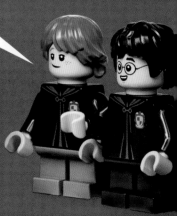

Gray ingot pieces are the same height as tiles

PLATFORM 9¾

Harry's come to catch the Hogwarts Express, and he's just realized he must run through a brick wall to reach Platform 9¾. Yikes! This build shows Ron safely through to the magical platform and Harry following him. To make it feel more like the real Kings Cross station in London, try adding train tracks alongside.

BUILD TIP

The simplest builds can be brought to life by well-chosen minifigures. Here, a character in a wizard's hat shows that Harry is entering the magical world.

LUGGAGE DASH

Build the travelers a wheeled cart each, then load them up with trunks, cases, and pets. This model has Harry pushing only half a cart. The other half has already disappeared into the wall.

Stickered tile platform sign

COME ON, HARRY... IT DOESN'T HURT.

Include jumper plates in the floor to pose minifigures on

Stack the cart with minifigure accessories or your own creations

ALL ABOARD!

Smooth stone floor made from tiles

Scabbers is always by Ron's side

Wheels attach in pairs underneath

RON'S CART

VANISHING ACT
The luggage on Harry's halfway-through cart is built right into the station wall. Hedwig in her cage will be the last of his precious cargo to make it through to Platform 9¾.

Two 1×1 round plates for Hedwig

Wall bricks surround the cart

Extend this arch for a larger station scene

I HOPE MY GLASSES DON'T BREAK!

These Muggles haven't noticed where Harry is going

This sign is a 2×2 square flag with two clips

1×5×4 arches for the wide railroad arches

Mix textured and regular bricks for realistic station walls

SIDE VIEW

Bricks build up the platform height

If you don't have train tracks, lay your own from plates and tiles

HOGWARTS EXPRESS INTERIOR

How excited do Harry and Ron look to be traveling on this handsome Hogwarts Express build? They're clearly the perfect companions to share a compartment. The model focuses on the train's comfortable interior. It's made of individual compartments so you can make your own train interior longer or shorter, as if by magic.

BUILD TIP

Research or rewatch moments from the Harry Potter films so you can build realistic details into your models. They will make your creations extra special.

COZY COMPARTMENTS

Phew... they caught the train! Hermione, Ron, and Harry relax on blue seats, their cases stowed on an overhead rack. A window gives a view of the landscape going by. To make things even cozier, add a ceiling and interior door.

If you don't have LEGO suitcases, build your own from plates and tiles

1×2 curved slopes shape the seat backs

Leave exposed studs to sit your minifigures on

Blue tiles for the carpeted compartment floor

Large window for enjoying the views (and losing chocolate frogs!)

REAR VIEW

TOP VIEW

Compartment walls are one stud wide

LUGGAGE RACK

There's plenty of storage space above each compartment's seats for young witches' and wizards' belongings. These racks are made from ladder pieces and tiles with bars. They attach sideways to studs in the walls.

1½×2×2 ladder on its side

1×1 round tile with bar

Wood panel above the window

THOSE PUMPKIN PASTIES SMELL SO GOOD!

TROLLEY IN TRANSIT

Your minifigures are probably listening for the sound of rattling wheels. That means the Honeydukes Express trolley is on its way. Load it up with colorful treats, and find a friendly trolley witch to push it.

1×1 transparent plates are wall lamps

Cauldron cakes with icing made from 1×1 plates with petals

Brown plates for the seat bases

Larger wheels are the backs of 2×2 round jumper plates

DURMSTRANG SHIP

What looks like a galleon but travels underwater, like a submarine? It's the Durmstrang ship, bringing students from that famous wizarding school on a visit to Hogwarts. Don't forget to add Durmstrang colors and elaborate details. If you do, headmaster Igor Karkaroff might have your minifigures scrubbing the deck.

HOGWARTS AHOY!

This build shows the ship after it has risen majestically from beneath the waves. Everything is shipshape, from the masts to the swiveling cannon. At the back is a raised poop deck. Durmstrang's star pupil, Viktor Krum, might stand here as the ship approaches Hogwarts.

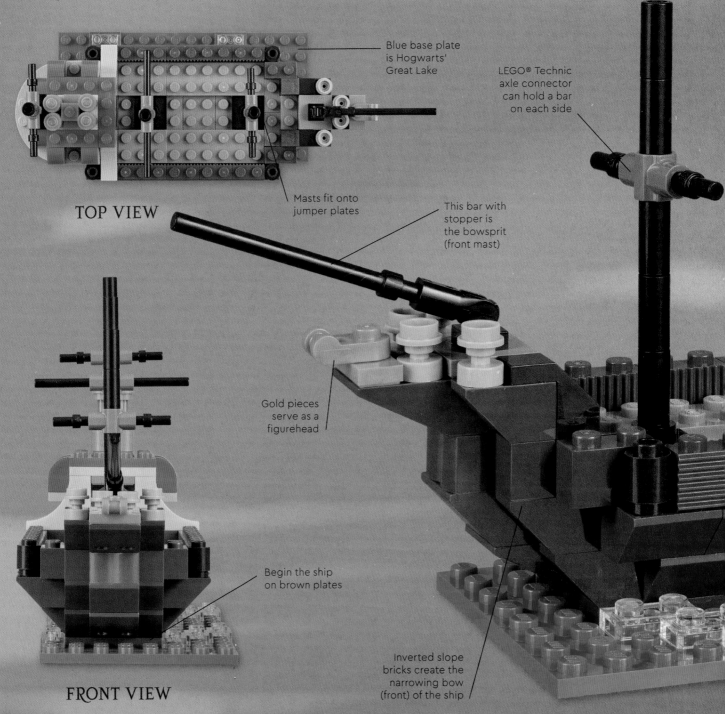

Blue base plate is Hogwarts' Great Lake

LEGO® Technic axle connector can hold a bar on each side

Masts fit onto jumper plates

TOP VIEW

This bar with stopper is the bowsprit (front mast)

Gold pieces serve as a figurehead

Begin the ship on brown plates

FRONT VIEW

Inverted slope bricks create the narrowing bow (front) of the ship

BUILD TIP

Building sails onto the ship at this scale could weigh down the masts and cause them to topple. If you decide to build at a bigger scale, try creating sails, too.

Masts are stacked candle elements

BELOW DECK

The ship's poop deck is built up in three layers, incorporating headlight brick windows and smooth curves on the first two. Golden lanterns adorn the smaller top level along with a small sail.

A bar connects these elements

The back of a 1×1 headlight brick has a square hole

Red is the color of the Durmstrang Institute

HAVE YOU BROUGHT YOUR SEA LEGS, HERMIONE?

1×2 ridged bricks look like wooden rails

Transparent pieces are ripples on the Great Lake

HOGWARTS GREAT HALL

From festive feasts to Dueling Club tussles, Hogwarts Great Hall has seen many dramatic moments. You don't need to build the whole hall to re-create them—small sections are enough to create a magical atmosphere. Here are some great ideas to set the scene for your favorite Great Hall moments.

BUILD TIP

Check the height and width of your minifigures before building doors and furniture for them. They are four studs tall (minus hair) and just under four studs wide.

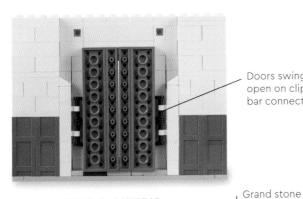

Doors swing open on clip and bar connections

REAR VIEW

IMPOSING DOOR

Brown LEGO pieces make the hall's heavy door and wall paneling look like solid oak. The brick walls are a bit uneven, just like real castle walls. Why not cover the cracks with school banners or portraits of former Hogwarts students?

Grand stone carvings above the double doors

TROLL IN THE DUNGEON!

Stacked 2×2×2 container boxes for the wood paneling

SIDE VIEW

Use a mix of tile colors for an ancient stone floor

Dumbledore's throne is taller than the rest

Armrests are 1×3 inverted arches

Light candles for a cozy ambience

Chair headrests are 1×2 triple slope pieces

Three 4×8 plates serve as the long tabletop

Gold horn is a water jug handle

HIGH TABLE

KEEP CALM, EVERYONE!

2×2 transparent dome is a glass dome at the base

LECTERN

TEACHERS' TABLE

Settle down now! Hogwarts teachers can see every student in the Hall from the elevated High Table. Build a throne chair in the middle for headmaster Professor Dumbledore, and a winged golden lectern for solemn speeches.

EAGLE FEATURES

The top of the lectern, where Dumbledore rests his speech notes, is shaped like an eagle spreading its wings. A 1×1 brick with four side studs holds the eagle's head, wings, and talons.

1×1 slope is the eagle's head

1×1 brick with four side studs

Transparent minifigure posing stand

1×1 plate with clip for the talons

Two 1×3×3 arches make pointed doorways

Lanterns light the way to the top floors

This level has an 8×8 plate base

THERE IS A STEP-BY-STEP GUIDE!

The walls with portraits in them are one stud wider

HOW DO I USE THE STAIRCASE?

Inverted slopes support the upper doorways

Attach any minifigure heads to jumper plates for animated portraits

Stone columns frame the doorways

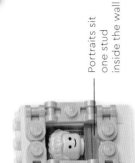

Build little shelves into the walls for candles

Staircase is stacked bricks with a top layer of plates and tiles

Try not to bump into "High Inquisitor" Dolores Umbridge on the stairs!

SIDE VIEW

Portraits sit one stud inside the wall

WALL PORTRAITS

Fashion frames out of any connecting gold pieces

This is the floor of the level above

MOVING STAIRS

Build this LEGO version of Hogwarts' Grand Staircase, complete with moving stairs. Will the stairs take your minifigures where they want to go, or confuse them by taking them to the wrong floor? For even more ups, downs, ins, and outs, try adding a second staircase or even a third.

JUMP TO IT!

The stairs attach to plates on the floor and landings, so they can be repositioned in various ways. Just make sure your minifigures always have an exit point. Don't leave them stranded on a landing near a grumpy wizard portrait.

SWIVELLING MOTION

The middle floor has turntable pieces that the bottom of the stairs can fit onto. This allows the staircase to smoothly swivel between doorways on the top floor. Hold on tight!

4×4 turntable has a base and a round plate top

COMMON ROOMS

Sometimes, a Hogwarts student just wants to hang out with others of their own house. That's when they head for their cozy common room. These builds show Gryffindor and Slytherin common rooms, but you could create a Ravenclaw or Hufflepuff one if that's your preferred house. Or even all four!

SPECIAL PIECE

The 1×4 double curved slope is useful for furniture building. The top of the backrests on the Gryffindor armchairs are shaped by this piece.

Wall torch fits onto a 1×1 plate with clip in the wall

Add classic castle touches like this stone window surround

Gryffindor's common room is messier than Slytherin's!

Brown 1×1 round plates are burning wood

Hedwig's pe is just three pieces

Chess piece is a microfigure

Dark-red rug matches the wall color

Chessboard is 1×1 tiles built onto the tabletop

I'LL TAKE YOU ON, RON!

GRYFFINDOR COMMON ROOM

The Gryffindor common room is decorated in warm red colors. There's a lattice window, books galore, and a cozy fire for Hedwig to snooze by. Would your minifigures care to join Ron in a game of wizard chess?

Gray 1×2×2 cat tails look like carved stone

Tall regular and corner slope bricks top the mantlepiece

Build bricks with side studs into the walls for 2×2 tile portraits to hang from

Add studious accessories to your scenes

2×4 oval round tiles make snug-looking rugs

SUMPTUOUS SLYTHERIN

In this green-hued common room, portraits of famous Slytherins hang proudly above a large, imposing fireplace. Best save your minifigures a seat on the black leather sofa before Crabbe and Goyle polish off all the doughnuts.

The bare base plates could be shaggy carpet

Shiny black pieces create a leathery finish

HOW DARE YOU DISMANTLE OUR FIREPLACE!

FIREBACK

Sometimes, showing the back of a piece can prove more effective than showing the front. The back wall or fireback of the fireplace is the reverse of a 4×12 plate. It attaches sideways to the exterior wall.

4×12 plate

1×1×1²⁄₃ brick with two side studs

MYSTERIOUS BATHROOM

Forget groaning pipework... Moaning Myrtle is the main hazard in this Hogwarts bathroom build. But ghostly Myrtle is the clue to a big secret. Somewhere in this bathroom is a hidden entrance to the legendary Chamber of Secrets! Have a go at building it and you'll be flushed with success.

6×6 round plates and 4×4 macaroni tiles top the pillar

The sink column is symmetrical

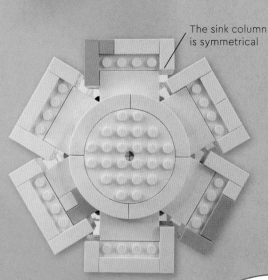

TOP VIEW

ELABORATE UNIT

Could there be more than water inside this fancy washbasin pillar? Try building a large, grand version at minifigure scale, with details that look like carved stone and leaky faucets that might just be holding back secrets.

Combine lots of smaller pieces for a carved effect

> BOO HOO...
> I'M HAUNTING
> A LOO!

BUILD TIP

This ancient girls' bathroom has been out of order for many years, so use a mixture of gray and white pieces to give its fixtures a gloomy, worn-out marble look.

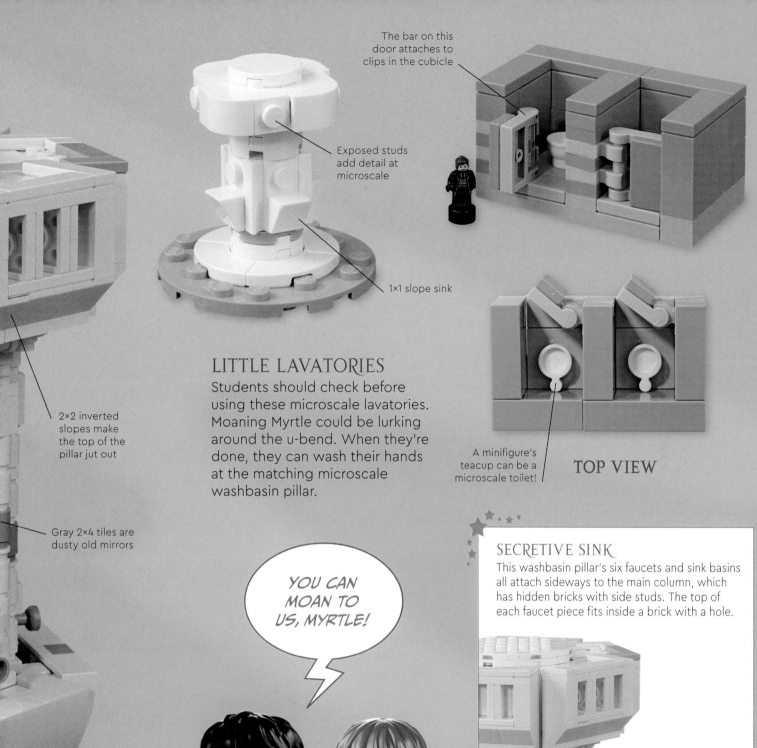

The bar on this door attaches to clips in the cubicle

Exposed studs add detail at microscale

1×1 slope sink

2×2 inverted slopes make the top of the pillar jut out

Gray 2×4 tiles are dusty old mirrors

LITTLE LAVATORIES

Students should check before using these microscale lavatories. Moaning Myrtle could be lurking around the u-bend. When they're done, they can wash their hands at the matching microscale washbasin pillar.

A minifigure's teacup can be a microscale toilet!

TOP VIEW

YOU CAN MOAN TO US, MYRTLE!

Three curved slopes shape each sink basin

SECRETIVE SINK

This washbasin pillar's six faucets and sink basins all attach sideways to the main column, which has hidden bricks with side studs. The top of each faucet piece fits inside a brick with a hole.

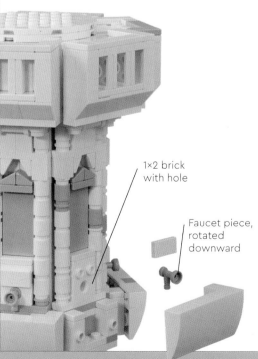

1×2 brick with hole

Faucet piece, rotated downward

WORLD CUP QUIDDITCH

Imagine being picked to play for your country in the Quidditch World Cup. It's enough to make your broomstick bristle with pride! You'll feel almost as proud when you build this set of Quidditch equipment. It has everything required for a world-class match. Or try building a mini World Cup Quidditch arena for a big game at a small scale.

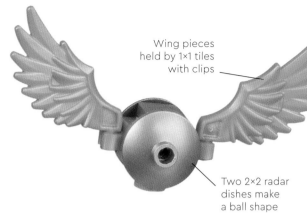

Wing pieces held by 1×1 tiles with clips

Two 2×2 radar dishes make a ball shape

GOLDEN SNITCH

KIT AND CABOODLE

A red Quaffle takes center stage in this box. The Bludgers are safely chained down, but the Beater's bat is ready to be grabbed when they are released. As for the Golden Snitch, it's already in full flight.

Red Quaffle is four 3×3×2 round corner bricks

SIDE VIEW

Two black sausage pieces form each handle

Four chain pieces hold down each Bludger

Two LEGO Technic pin connectors for the Beater's bat handle

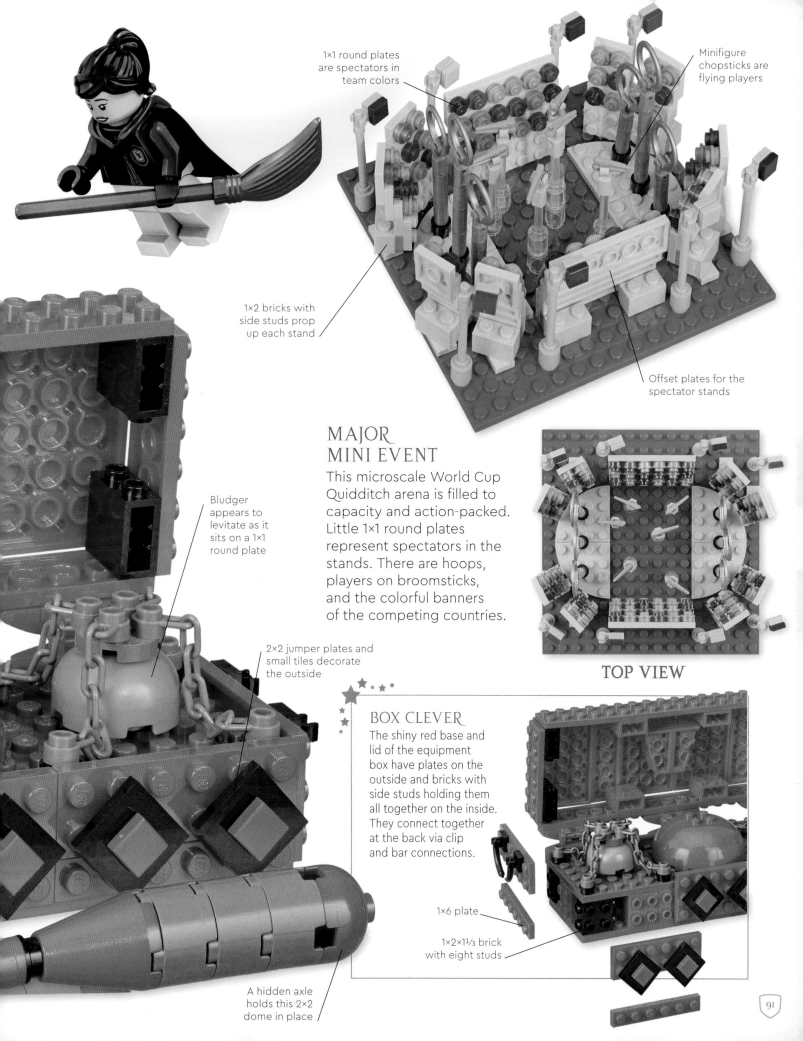

1×1 round plates
are spectators in
team colors

Minifigure
chopsticks are
flying players

1×2 bricks with
side studs prop
up each stand

Offset plates for the
spectator stands

MAJOR MINI EVENT

This microscale World Cup
Quidditch arena is filled to
capacity and action-packed.
Little 1×1 round plates
represent spectators in the
stands. There are hoops,
players on broomsticks,
and the colorful banners
of the competing countries.

Bludger
appears to
levitate as it
sits on a 1×1
round plate

2×2 jumper plates and
small tiles decorate
the outside

TOP VIEW

BOX CLEVER

The shiny red base and
lid of the equipment
box have plates on the
outside and bricks with
side studs holding them
all together on the inside.
They connect together
at the back via clip
and bar connections.

1×6 plate

1×2×1⅓ brick
with eight studs

A hidden axle
holds this 2×2
dome in place

91

SWEDISH SHORT-SNOUT DRAGON

Dragons may be tricky to tame, but they're much less difficult to build. Pick your favorite fire-breathing beastie from the Harry Potter movies and build it from your LEGO collection. This is a Swedish Short-Snout. Be careful as you turn to the next page: there's a Chinese Fireball lurking there!

SIDE VIEW

SWEDISH SHORT-SNOUT

Cedric Diggory faced a Swedish Short-Snout in the Triwizard Tournament, and got a bit of a scorching for his efforts. This snub-nosed dragon breathes blue fire, so add some flames if you like.

Ninja sword blades create the outstretched wings

Moving tail is built in sections connected by ball and socket plates

UH-OH... I THINK IT'S SPOTTED ME!

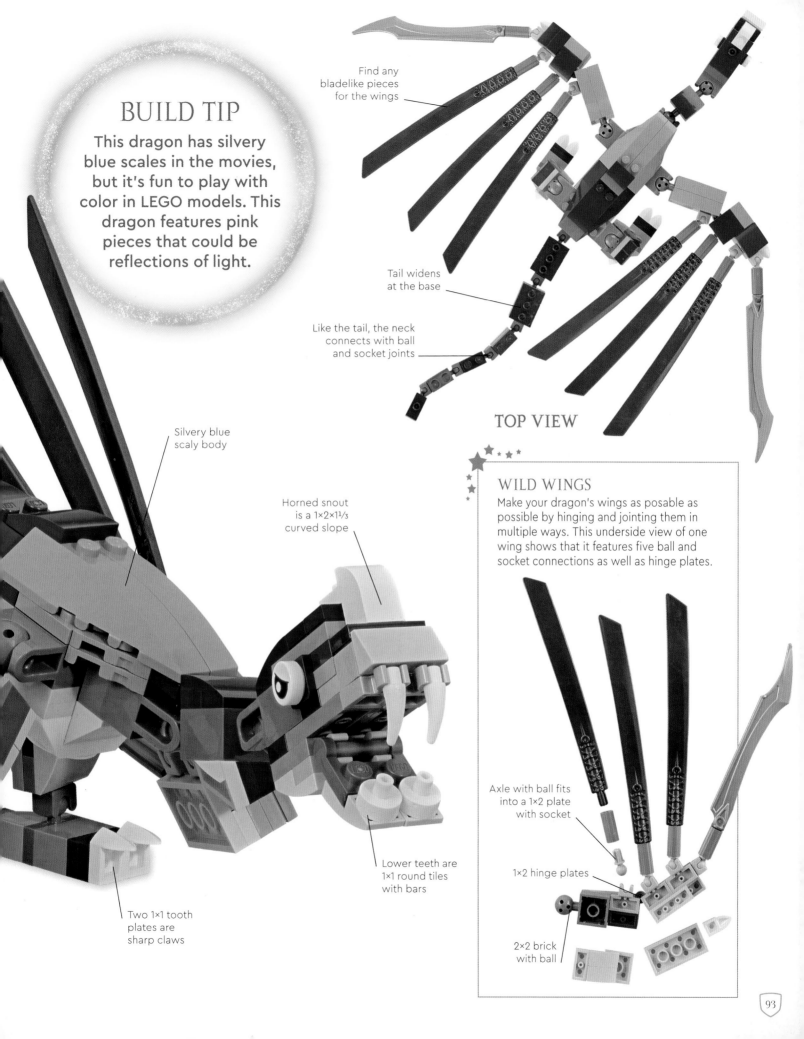

BUILD TIP

This dragon has silvery blue scales in the movies, but it's fun to play with color in LEGO models. This dragon features pink pieces that could be reflections of light.

Find any bladelike pieces for the wings

Tail widens at the base

Like the tail, the neck connects with ball and socket joints

TOP VIEW

Silvery blue scaly body

Horned snout is a 1×2×1⅓ curved slope

Lower teeth are 1×1 round tiles with bars

Two 1×1 tooth plates are sharp claws

WILD WINGS

Make your dragon's wings as posable as possible by hinging and jointing them in multiple ways. This underside view of one wing shows that it features five ball and socket connections as well as hinge plates.

Axle with ball fits into a 1×2 plate with socket

1×2 hinge plates

2×2 brick with ball

CHINESE FIREBALL DRAGON

Grab your LEGO pieces and let your imagination take flight with another Triwizard Tournament dragon build. Take inspiration from these models or look at other dragons of the wizarding world. You could build a Hungarian Horntail; a Welsh Green; or Hagrid's Norwegian Ridgeback hatchling, Norberta.

SPECIAL PIECE

The tiny horn that forms the dragon's fangs and spikes on this model has so many uses. It has a small bar on the end that plugs snugly into open studs.

HOLY SMOKES!

CHINESE FIREBALL

This snorting scarlet dragon was drawn by Viktor Krum as his first challenge when the Triwizard Tournament came to Hogwarts. How does it get its name? From the flames that emerge from its nostrils. Look out!

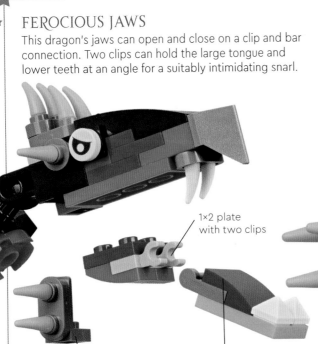

Orange spikes crown the head

Snub snout is a 1×2 double slope

Horn piece fangs hang from open studs

FEROCIOUS JAWS

This dragon's jaws can open and close on a clip and bar connection. Two clips can hold the large tongue and lower teeth at an angle for a suitably intimidating snarl.

1×2 plate with two clips

This spiked section fits just behind the jaw

2×2 curved slope tongue

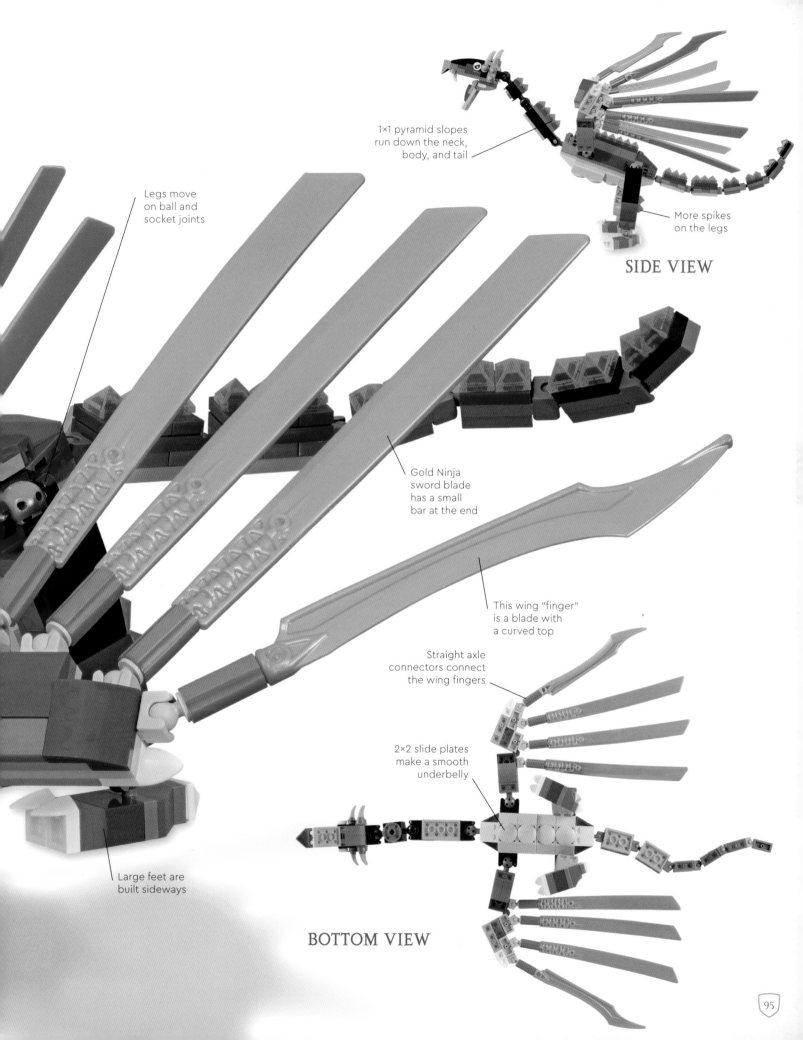

Legs move
on ball and
socket joints

1×1 pyramid slopes
run down the neck,
body, and tail

More spikes
on the legs

SIDE VIEW

Gold Ninja
sword blade
has a small
bar at the end

This wing "finger"
is a blade with
a curved top

Straight axle
connectors connect
the wing fingers

2×2 slide plates
make a smooth
underbelly

Large feet are
built sideways

BOTTOM VIEW

WEASLEY WEDDING

Bill Weasley and Fleur Delacour have tied the knot! Wish the magical couple all the best with this wedding party build, set in a romantic, purple-draped gazebo. If you'd like to include more guests, it's easy to create a larger scene. Just make sure you don't invite any Death Eaters by mistake!

BUILD TIP

Building something as big as a wedding gazebo can feel daunting but this build shows that making small sections of a scene can create the right atmosphere.

1×2 Inverted curved slopes are draped fabric

Stacked 1×1 bricks for the gazebo supports

AS IF THERE WEREN'T ENOUGH WEASLEYS!

Tiered cake stand can spin around on bars

Connect more base plates to extend your scene

TOP TABLE

Create matching tables and chairs for your wedding scene. Peek below the purple tablecloth to see how the table base is built from five plates and four candle legs. The chairs are also fashioned from just a handful of pieces.

6×6 round plate tabletop

Ladder plate backrest

1×2 tile with bar chair legs

Minifigure candle accessory

1×1 round tile with bar

1×1 plates with petals are flower decorations

This minifigure whip accessory makes a swan-neck lantern

GARDEN PARTY

The Weasleys set up a gazebo in their garden especially for the wedding party. It's got a buffet, glasses for a toast, and a dance floor ready for those strange wizarding dances. Have your minifigures learned the steps?

Which Weasley will be first to the buffet table?

Triangle tile is a napkin

Bricks look like an overhanging tablecloth

Fresh leaves and flowers adorn the tables

SLUG & JIGGERS

Are your minifigures shopping for premium potion ingredients? Then build Slug & Jiggers Apothecary in Diagon Alley for them to visit. There are weird and wonderful things behind the shop's purple-painted windows, but witches and wizards might want to hold their noses before they step inside. Pickled blowfly eggs, anyone?

SHOP WINDOWS

The large bay windows on the ground floor are built sideways from layers of one-stud-wide plates. A two-stud-wide plate at one end secures the window to sideways pieces on the building.

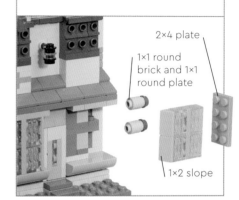

2×4 plate

1×1 round brick and 1×1 round plate

1×2 slope

Some of the shop's wares are hanging outside it

EVERYTHING'S IN STOCK

Ingredients sell like hot dung-cakes in this popular shop. Build a few floors above the shop for the full-to-bursting stockrooms, and lanterns to help customers find the place in the dark.

Rows of headlight bricks look like lattice windows

SIDE VIEW

Gray base plate for the cobbled pavement

WHAT'S LUCIUS MALFOY UP TO?

Purple paintwork hints at the magic inside

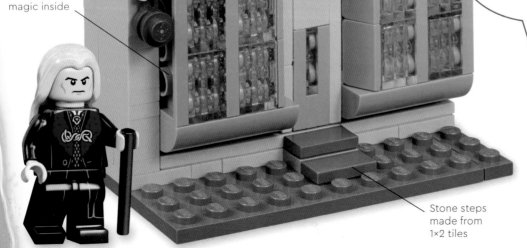

Stone steps made from 1×2 tiles

This arched piece is often seen as a mudguard on LEGO vehicles

Fit together plant and vine pieces for overgrown foliage

Baby mandrake stored in a soundproof dome

Naturally shed owl feathers are also a potion ingredient

There are plants growing inside the shelves

Small pot is a 1×1 tile and 1×1 round plate

ON THE SHELF

The shop's interior is higgledy-piggledy, so make shelves mismatched in size and shape. Bottles and jars sit on the shelves, while plants can hang on the outside. You could offer feathers, toadstools, and unicorn horns for sale, too.

HERBOLOGY SHELF

Green arrowheads are hanging plants

Smaller ledges for tiny ingredients

POTIONS SHELF

1×1 plate with petals is a foot

Log bricks make sturdy wooden shelves

1×1 cheese slope is a wedge of an ingredient

BUILD TIP

Anything goes when it comes to building the unusual wares of this shop. Snap any pieces together to make quirky potion bottles and mystery ingredients.

INGREDIENTS SHELF

99

Use a mixture of browns for aging wood

END VIEW

THE COVERED BRIDGE

When crossing the Covered Bridge, your minifigures must step carefully. There's no telling who they'll meet—maybe even You-Know-Who. This ancient structure spans a ravine between Hogwarts Clock Tower and the Stone Circle in the school grounds. It's old and rickety, but that's not the biggest danger. Explosive events have happened here!

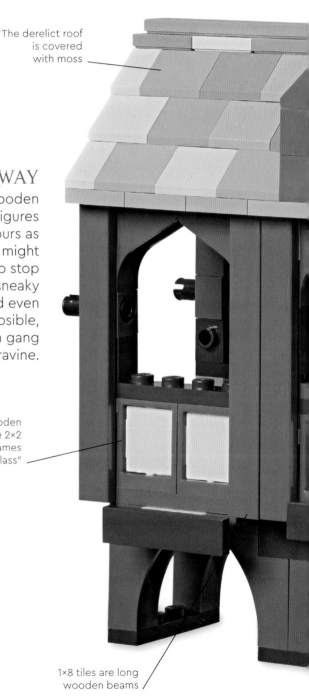

The derelict roof is covered with moss

WOODEN WALKWAY

The longer the wooden bridge, the more minifigures will fit onto it. Make yours as long as you like. You might need them to stop Voldemort's sneaky Snatchers. You could even make a section collapsible, and send the grim gang tumbling into the ravine.

SECTION OF BRIDGE

Three LEGO Technic pins connect each section

Wooden panels are 2×2 window frames with tan "glass"

★ ★ ★ ★
★
★ ★

DORMER WINDOW

Small windows jut out from the sloping roof of the Covered Bridge. Build them directly onto the roof base using a 1×4 arch, 1×1 bricks, and slopes.

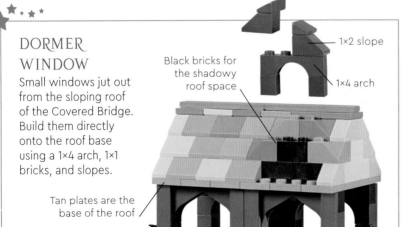

Black bricks for the shadowy roof space

1×2 slope

1×4 arch

Tan plates are the base of the roof

1×8 tiles are long wooden beams

2×2 jumper plates and narrow tiles top the roof

BEST NOT COME THIS WAY, NEVILLE. IT'S A SHEER DROP!

Slope bricks create the roof tiles

BUILD TIP

This bridge design is modular, which means it is built in small sections that connect together. Modular building is a good way to build long or tall objects or scenes.

Wooden stilts hold the bridge far above the ravine below

Two 1×3×2 arches frame each opening

SECRET PASSAGES

What's Harry up to? He's sneaking to Hogsmeade Village through a secret passage he spotted on the Marauder's Map. Help Harry out by building the passage he needs to sneak through, but be careful... don't let crabby caretaker Filch catch Harry. Try building other secret passages, too. Maybe there's one that leads to the school kitchens!

SPECIAL PIECE

This wall includes a few cleverly placed 1×1 bricks with open side studs. Incorporate some of these elements into your walls so you can attach candles, critters, and plants to them.

Candle is a 1×1 round plate with open stud

1×2 inverted slope bricks form the wall arches

Make your section of wall as long as you like

Gray tiles look like a stone floor

This alcove is a regular wall

WHERE'S THE DOOR?

That alcove on the left looks just like any other in the dark, candlelit Hogwarts hallway. Don't be fooled. Push that part of the wall and a hidden door swings open, leading to the secret passage.

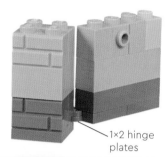

MOVING WALLS

The hallway wall is two studs deep. The rear part of the wall has built-in hinge plates on one side so a section of the wall can swing open like a door.

1×1 round plate with bar is a candle holder

1×2 hinge plates

REAR VIEW (DOOR)

This spider found the secret passageway first!

Include a candle so this swinging section blends in with the other walls

The cobweb clips to 1×1 bricks with bars

REAR VIEW (PASSAGE)

Mix up shades of gray for an ancient brick effect

Plants are growing out of the walls

Build on wider plates for a sturdy base

WHO'S THERE, MRS. NORRIS? I HEAR FOOTSTEPS!

BLOW AWAY THE COBWEBS

Beyond the hall doorway, a giant cobweb covers the passage. Is Hogsmeade just past the cobweb, or is this just the beginning? You could build a really long passage, with a series of doorways and tunnels for your minifigures to pass through.

FORBIDDEN FOREST

If Hagrid asked you to "follow the spiders" into the Forbidden Forest, would you go? Harry and Ron did, but at least one of them is already regretting it. Build a LEGO version of this dark, dangerous woodland that borders the grounds of Hogwarts, filling it with spiders, gnarly trees, and other creepy things.

2×2 round plate secures the eyes

TOP VIEW

4×4 triple curved wedge shapes the abdomen

ARAGOG

This giant Acromantula spider is Hagrid's buddy, but Harry and Ron aren't sure it wants to be theirs! Give your Aragog movable pincers so it can reach out and grab minifigures who venture too close.

Pedipalps (small front limbs) are made from bar holders with clips

Small bar with stopper for the tapering leg end

⭐⭐⭐ LEG LAYER

Lift up Aragog's rounded cephalothorax (its head and body) and you can see that it starts off square, on a 4×4 plate base. Each leg clips to a rounded 1×1 plate with bar on this base plate.

4×4 radar dish starts off the upper layers

1×1 rounded plate with bar

Bar holder with clip

BUILD TIP

Grab your leafiest elements to fill your forest trees with dense foliage. Make simple branches by sandwiching leaf pieces between round trunk bricks.

Layer up 3×4 leaves for the treetop

5×6 leaf pieces have lots of open studs

×2×1⅓ curved lope tree root

Vine pieces hang from open studs

Sturdy 2×2 round bricks for the trunk base

Small round plates are plants and leaves on the forest floor

I THINK IT'S TIME TO LEAVE NOW, RON.

WHO'S HIDING HERE?

Tall, leafy trees loom over a forest floor teeming with Aragog's hungry children. Why not expand the scene by adding some other rumored residents? Werewolves, Thestrals, and even Death Eaters are said to lurk here.

Don't trip over these 1×1 round plate stones!

REAR VIEW

105

MICROSCALE HOGWARTS

A microscale model is one that's smaller than minifigure scale. These tiny Hogwarts builds are good examples, but you can "microscale" any Harry Potter location you like. There won't be much room for detail, so pick your pieces wisely. The wizarding world spell for making things smaller—Reducio!— would have made this challenge a lot easier!

IT LOOKS SO SMALL FROM UP HERE!

SPECIAL PIECE

The unicorn horn piece is not a one-trick pony! It makes a great spire in micro architecture. How else could you use it? The small bar at one end plugs into an open stud.

This longer spire is a unicorn horn and 1×1 cone

Two 1×1 slopes form the roof of the Great Hall

SIDE VIEW

SMALLEST OF ALL?

This itsy-bitsy build uses just a handful of pieces, yet the wings and spires make it instantly recognizable as Hogwarts. Do you think you could make an even smaller version of the School of Witchcraft and Wizardry?

This 1×2 brick is the Clock Tower building

The Great Lake is one blue 4×6 plate

Stacked 1×1 round plates are the viaduct

Dumbledore's office is in this small turret

SIDE VIEW

DINKY DETAILS

A slightly larger microbuild will give you a few more opportunities for detail. Now you can add doors, windows, pillars, walkways, lawns, and extra spires. Make the rocks more complicated and the lake bigger, too.

GREAT DETAIL

At this scale, the Great Hall has ornate pillars. They're built sideways from plates with bars in between gray plates— one of which has a clip that attaches to a bar on Gryffindor Tower.

1×2 plate with clip

The hall sits on smooth tiles

Ridged round bricks add detail to this tower

The Clock Tower now has bigger spires and an archway

1×2/2×2 bracket plates form the rectangular shape of the Great Hall

Neat lawns surround the Clock Tower

Tiny boathouse on the rocks

1×4×2 spindled fence viaduct

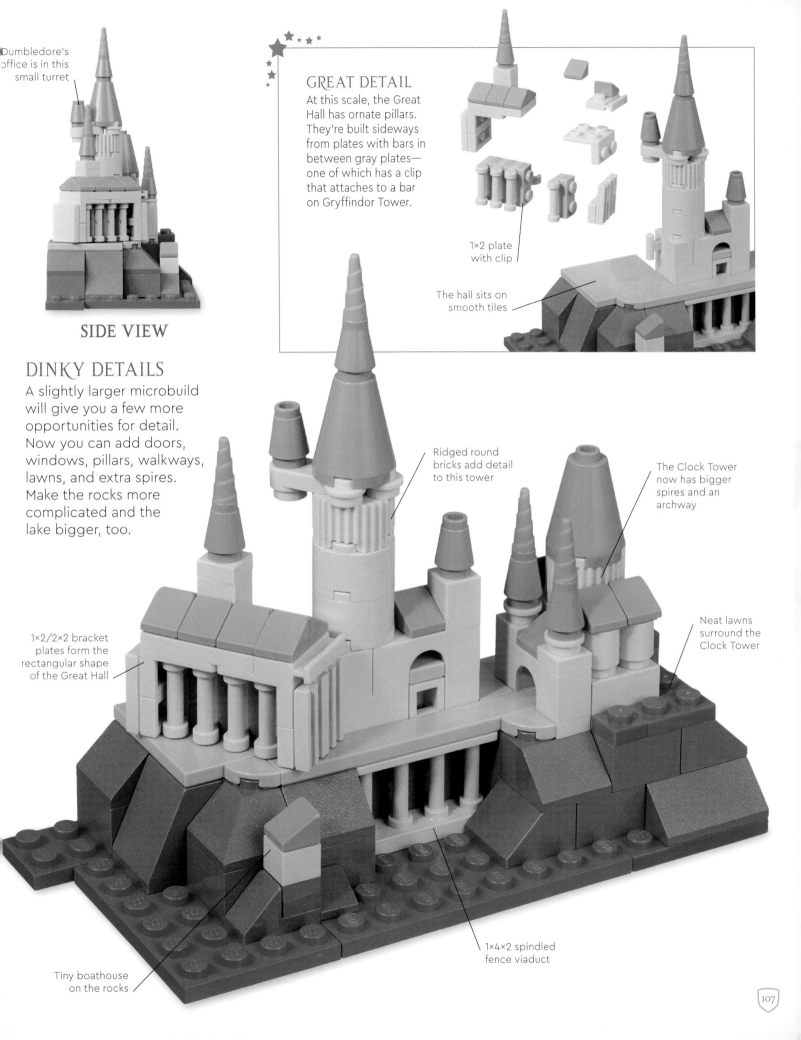

MICROSCALE SCENES

Your microscale builds must be simple but unmistakable, so use shapes and colors as clues. The hoops on a Quidditch pitch are an instant giveaway, and who could mistake the bright red Hogwarts Express for an everyday commuter train? Try building other Harry Potter scenes, items, and characters in microscale.

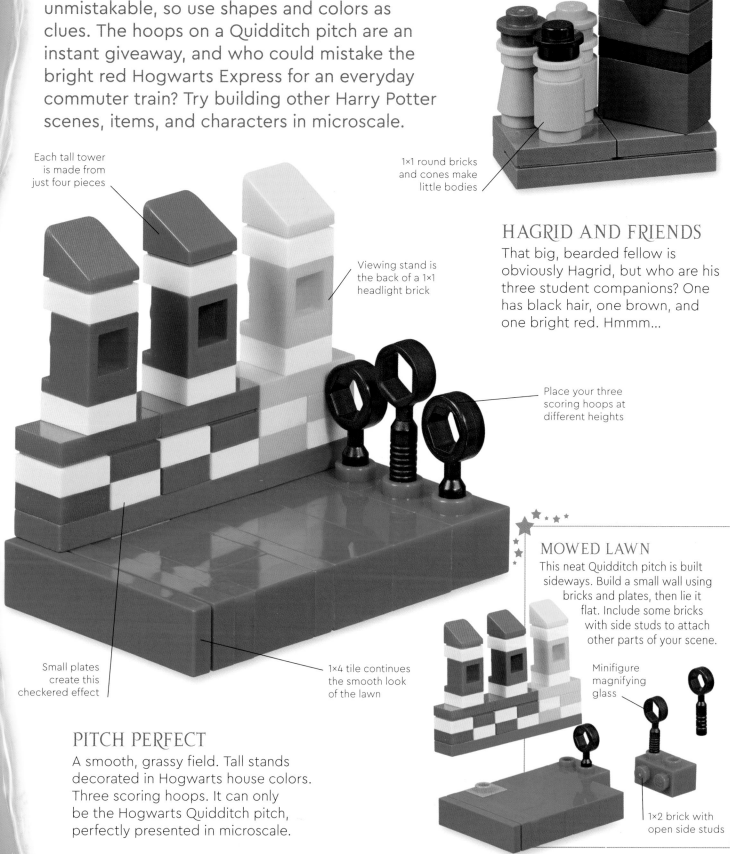

Bushy beard is a 1×1 vertical tooth plate

1×1 round bricks and cones make little bodies

Each tall tower is made from just four pieces

Viewing stand is the back of a 1×1 headlight brick

HAGRID AND FRIENDS

That big, bearded fellow is obviously Hagrid, but who are his three student companions? One has black hair, one brown, and one bright red. Hmmm...

Place your three scoring hoops at different heights

Small plates create this checkered effect

1×4 tile continues the smooth look of the lawn

MOWED LAWN

This neat Quidditch pitch is built sideways. Build a small wall using bricks and plates, then lie it flat. Include some bricks with side studs to attach other parts of your scene.

Minifigure magnifying glass

1×2 brick with open side studs

PITCH PERFECT

A smooth, grassy field. Tall stands decorated in Hogwarts house colors. Three scoring hoops. It can only be the Hogwarts Quidditch pitch, perfectly presented in microscale.

STATIONARY TRAIN

Here, the Hogwarts Express is waiting by the unmistakable arches of Platform 9¾ at Kings Cross station in London. Including a bit of background will give context to your microscale items.

REAR VIEW

This 1×2/1×2 inverted bracket holds up a tile

BUILD TIP

Microbuilds only use a few pieces, but that doesn't make them easy to build. Creating features like these railroad arches can take a lot of skill, so look closely at the pictures.

Tiny transparent late windows for taking in the view

Grand railroad arch is a 1×4×2 arch

1×1 round plates are train wheels

ALL ABOARD! (IF YOU CAN FIT IN.)

ENGINE ENGINEERING

The engine is made from three headlight bricks lying on their sides. The wheels plug into their undersides, while plates and tiles fit onto the single studs on their fronts.

Funnel is an upside-down 1×1 round tile with bar

1×1 headlight brick

One train wheel fits onto this jumper plate

109

CAMPING OUT

Are you a happy camper? Then help Harry and his friends set up their gear at the Quidditch World Cup campsite. Fans flock to this popular sporting event, so build a whole field full of tents if you wish. Just remember your minifigures must respect other campsite users. No loud chatting or casting spells after dark!

BUILD TIP

The top of the tent is not actually connected. Clip and bar connections hold the tent's sides at an angle from the bottom, and the sides rest on each other at the top.

4×8 inverted tiles make the sides or walls of the tent

USEFUL EQUIPMENT

A campfire by the tent is ideal for keeping witches and wizards warm. What other equipment might they need? Enchanted tent pegs and a magical mallet might come in handy. And a mini cauldron for that fire, obviously.

1×2 plate with bar clicks into a 1×1 tile with clip

2×8 plates hold up the tent's sides

Add leaves and green plates for overgrown grass

SIDE VIEW

Two 1×3 slope bricks look like an unzipped door

Ice-cream piece is billowing smoke

Chairs are 2×2 driving seats on top of 2×2 round plates

Place delectable treats on the table

TENT INTERIOR

Plant pot is a 2×2 inverted dome

TENT SWEET TENT
Enchanted tents are bigger on the inside, so Harry and Ron can spread out and enjoy a snack by the wood-burning stove. They even have room for a houseplant in their tent. Don't worry... it isn't a Venomous Tentacula.

INCENDIO!

ROARING FIRE
This cozy wood-burning stove is built upwards from a 2×2 round plate base. Its large flame is contained within a window piece, and the smoke puffs out of a chimney made from four tiny, connecting black elements.

1×2×2 window

Half pin holds the flame

Build a hearth from plates and tiles

SPECIAL PIECE
Bricks with holes can hold pin, half pin, and bar pieces. Including elements like this in your models will help you build sideways or add moving parts.

Just one LEGO Technic axle connector with bars can make a campfire

CHAPTER THREE

ITEMS FOR MUGGLES

Don't feel down if don't have any magical powers. Try conjuring up these very useful Harry Potter-themed builds... they'll bring a little magic to your everyday world. They're stylish, fun, and every one is approved for use by Muggles!

BUILD YOUR OWN WAND

Can't get to Ollivanders Wand Shop? Never mind, just custom-build your own LEGO® wand. Be inspired by the wands in the Harry Potter films or design your own to suit your personality, but remember... your wand chooses you, not the other way around. The LEGO pieces you have may be trying to tell you something.

A TWIRL OF WANDS

Here are the wands of some famous and infamous magic-makers. Can you spot Voldemort's pale, bony-looking wand and Dumbledore's notched wood wand?

These long tiles are built sideways onto bricks with side studs

Two 1×1×5 bricks form this section

1×1 cone tip

Thin black wand looks like lacquered wood

Wood-grain printed 1×1 tiles add texture to this handle

1×2 grille plates suggest engraved silver

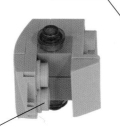

HARRY POTTER

LUCIUS MALFOY

SORRY... THE SHOP'S CLOSED FOR A SPELL.

SNAKE FOR A SNAKE

Lucius Malfoy's wand has a silver handle shaped like a snake's head with shiny emerald-green eyes. There's a hidden bar that connects the wand to the eerie handle.

1×1 brick with open stud (and side studs)

1×1 round plate fang

Bar piece threads through multiple elements

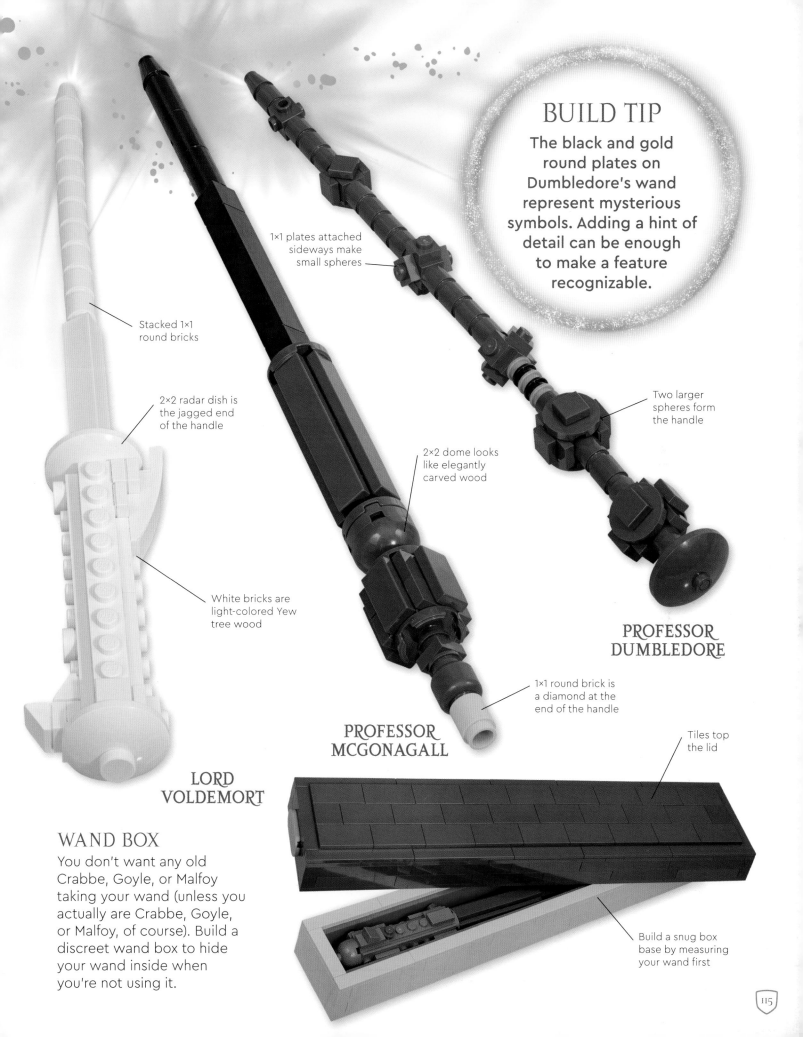

BUILD TIP

The black and gold round plates on Dumbledore's wand represent mysterious symbols. Adding a hint of detail can be enough to make a feature recognizable.

Stacked 1×1 round bricks

1×1 plates attached sideways make small spheres

2×2 radar dish is the jagged end of the handle

Two larger spheres form the handle

2×2 dome looks like elegantly carved wood

White bricks are light-colored Yew tree wood

PROFESSOR DUMBLEDORE

PROFESSOR MCGONAGALL

1×1 round brick is a diamond at the end of the handle

LORD VOLDEMORT

Tiles top the lid

WAND BOX

You don't want any old Crabbe, Goyle, or Malfoy taking your wand (unless you actually are Crabbe, Goyle, or Malfoy, of course). Build a discreet wand box to hide your wand inside when you're not using it.

Build a snug box base by measuring your wand first

ANIMAL COMPANIONS

At Hogwarts, animals are more than pets. They're true companions, with magical wisdom of their own. New students are invited to bring a cat, toad, or owl, but these aren't the only animals they'll meet there. Why not build a Magical Menagerie to rival the famous pet shop on Diagon Alley?

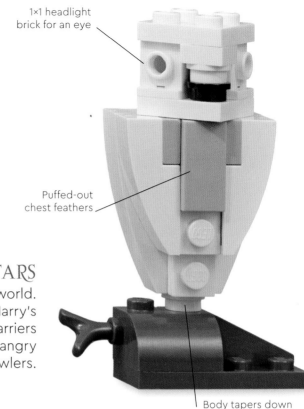

1×1 headlight brick for an eye

Puffed-out chest feathers

Body tapers down to one-stud wide

HOOTING STARS

Owls are important in the wizarding world. Some are companion animals, like Harry's Hedwig. Others are magical mail-carriers who deliver letters, packages, and angry voice messages called Howlers.

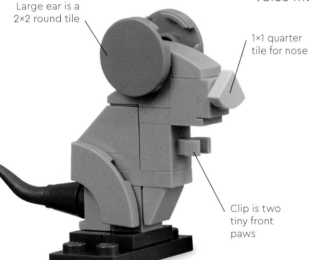

Large ear is a 2×2 round tile

1×1 quarter tile for nose

Clip is two tiny front paws

MYSTIC MICE

Many mice are resident in the nooks and crannies of the hallowed halls and classrooms of Hogwarts. One place you'll never find them is the Owlery. They don't want to be Hedwig's dinner!

Nose is the top edge of a heart tile

CLEVER KITTIES

Cats, such as Hermione's Crookshanks, are usually friendly and helpful to magical folk. The only unfriendly cat is Mrs. Norris. She regularly alerts grumpy Hogwarts caretaker Argus Filch to out-of-bounds students.

1×1 plate with ring is a back paw

One 1×2 plate with rail makes two front paws

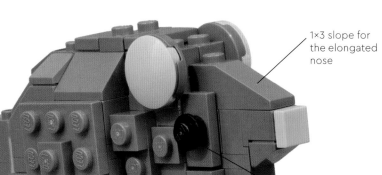

SPECIAL PIECES

The rat's long tail is made from two elements usually found on LEGO dinosaurs: the dinosaur tail tip and the mid-section, which has a pin at one end.

1×3 slope for the elongated nose

Small eye is a 1×1 round plate on a 1×2 jumper plate

Exposed studs suggest shaggy fur

PACK A RAT

Ron didn't really want a pet rat, but he inherited scruffy old Scabbers from his older brother. Little did Ron know that Scabbers was hiding a big secret beneath his furry coat!

ANYONE SEEN SCABBERS?

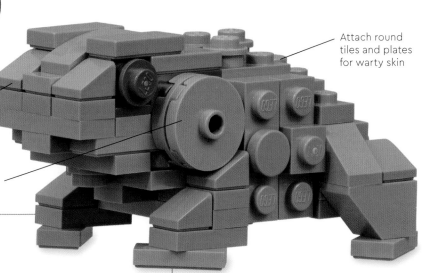

Attach round tiles and plates for warty skin

Small slopes create the rounded body shape

2×2 round jumper plate is a large gland

SPOT THE STUDS

Lots of the animals on this page have hidden sideways studs built into their bodies. Can you spot where? The toad's eyes, glands, and rear end attach in this way.

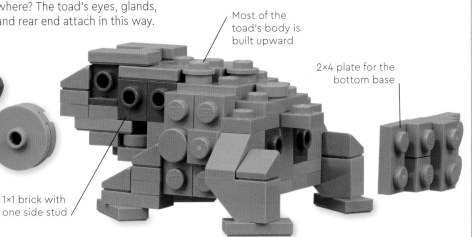

Most of the toad's body is built upward

2×4 plate for the bottom base

1×1 brick with one side stud

TOADALLY MAGICAL

Toads aren't particularly popular with modern students, but laid-back amphibians remain recommended pets at Hogwarts. Despite toads being rather slow, Neville has lost his pet toad, Trevor, numerous times.

WEASLEY FAMILY CLOCK

Where's Arthur Weasley? Happily driving his Ford Anglia or in mortal peril? The hands of this Weasley family clock are minifigures that turn to show where each member is at any given time. There are really nine Weasleys, so make a bigger clock if you like. Can you make a clock like this for your own family or friends?

LOCATION, LOCATION

Places and scenarios on this magical clock include at home, in transit, at school, playing Quidditch, in the Owlery, and in mortal peril. Build a symbol for each one—then put the many Weasleys where you want them.

The Weasleys' flying Ford Anglia represents the family in transit

Tiny ver. of The Burrow

Each location sits on a 4×4 plate

HANDS DOWN

The minifigure clock hands can turn individually thanks to a cleverly built dial. Start with a 4×4 square turntable base and add a 4×4 round brick on top. Add layers of plates for one hand before adding another turntable base on top.

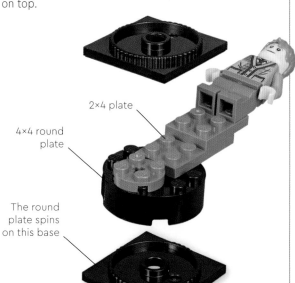

2×4 plate

4×4 round plate

The round plate spins on this base

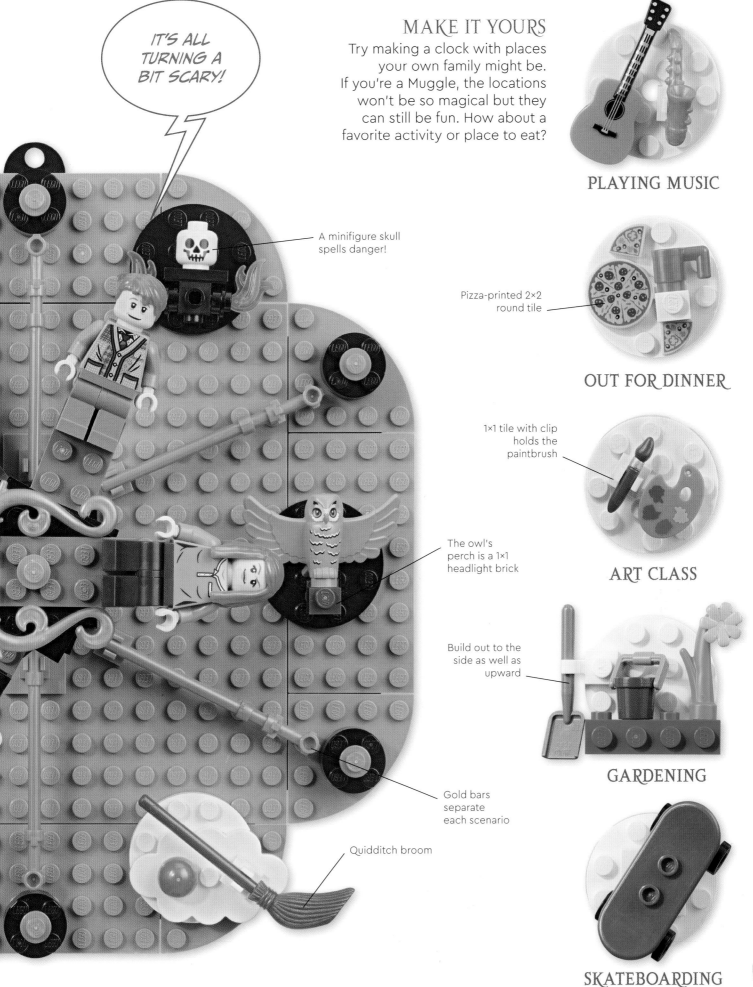

IT'S ALL TURNING A BIT SCARY!

MAKE IT YOURS
Try making a clock with places your own family might be. If you're a Muggle, the locations won't be so magical but they can still be fun. How about a favorite activity or place to eat?

PLAYING MUSIC

A minifigure skull spells danger!

Pizza-printed 2×2 round tile

OUT FOR DINNER

1×1 tile with clip holds the paintbrush

ART CLASS

The owl's perch is a 1×1 headlight brick

Build out to the side as well as upward

GARDENING

Gold bars separate each scenario

Quidditch broom

SKATEBOARDING

FAMILY TREE

Celebrate the generations with a LEGO family tree. The two shown here are for magical families, but don't forget your own Muggle kin. Your grandad might not be a great wizard or your auntie an Animagus, but they would be proud to pose on your tree in minifigure form.

BUILD TIP

To make your family tree as stable as possible, build round plates at regular intervals into the trunk. They will stop the bricks between them from collapsing.

Add green leaves to the branches if yours is a spring or summer tree

If you don't have arch pieces, you could make a branch shape with staggered bricks

ROOTING FOR HARRY

This Potter family tree shows Harry when he's all grown up. That's him on the middle branch with wife Ginny. His parents are at the top, and his kids, James, Albus, and Lily, are at the bottom.

Put each generation on a new branch

4×12 plate for a large branch

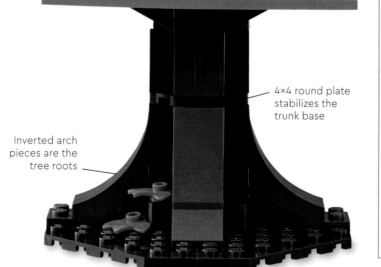

4×4 round plate stabilizes the trunk base

Inverted arch pieces are the tree roots

TREETOP LAYER

Each generational branch of the tree is supported by a sturdy layer of bricks built into the trunk. The top branch has log bricks and a 2×2 round brick under the minifigure plinth.

1×2 log brick

Layers that don't support branches are built differently

YOUR FAMILY TREE

Are you part of a big family? The Weasleys certainly are. You'll need a lot of room on the branches if you create their family tree. Build jumper-plate plinths for each family member so you know no one's missing.

WHERE ARE BILL AND CHARLIE?

THEY'RE TOO LATE... WE REMOVED THE LADDER!

4×6 plate is just right for two minifigures

Don't forget animal family members

Two 1×2 jumper plates hold each family member

The Weasley children need three branches to stand on

You could add another branch layer here for the Weasley children's children

Mix shades of brown for a natural look

Build onto a wide base plate to keep the tree upright

SIDE VIEW

WAND RACK

The trouble with wands is that they often go wandering. It's not because they are enchanted. It's because they're just the right shape to slip between sofa cushions or roll to the back of a drawer. Build this LEGO rack and never wave goodbye to your wands again.

SPECIAL PIECE

The A-shaped wedge plate is an important piece for this build. Four on each side create space for the compartments and hold the side plates in place.

Leave the back plain or decorate that, too

The plate colors at the back are the opposite to the front

REAR VIEW

GREATEST FAN

The rack has an elegant fan shape that echoes the Wizarding World logo. How many wand models will your rack display? Maybe you could have different-colored compartments to hold Gryffindor, Slytherin, Ravenclaw, and Hufflepuff wands.

I'M A FAN, TOO... OF VOLDEMORT.

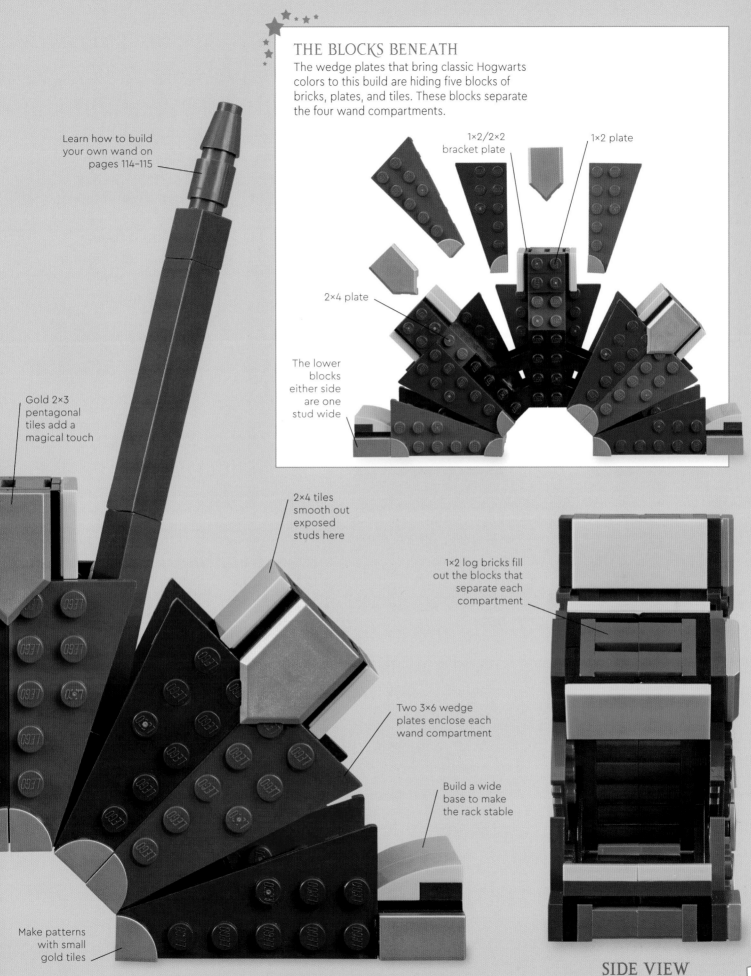

THE BLOCKS BENEATH

The wedge plates that bring classic Hogwarts colors to this build are hiding five blocks of bricks, plates, and tiles. These blocks separate the four wand compartments.

1×2/2×2 bracket plate

1×2 plate

2×4 plate

The lower blocks either side are one stud wide

Learn how to build your own wand on pages 114–115

Gold 2×3 pentagonal tiles add a magical touch

2×4 tiles smooth out exposed studs here

1×2 log bricks fill out the blocks that separate each compartment

Two 3×6 wedge plates enclose each wand compartment

Build a wide base to make the rack stable

Make patterns with small gold tiles

SIDE VIEW

123

CHRISTMAS TREE DECORATIONS

Spruce up your Christmas tree with some Hogwarts-themed ornaments. You don't have to copy the ones here. Yours could be a seasonal Sorting Hat, Aragog the Acromantula, or a Hogwarts acceptance letter. Or perhaps you know a Gryffindor, Slytherin, Ravenclaw, or Hufflepuff who would love some house-themed decorations as a gift.

SPECIAL PIECE

This special 2×2 tile has a hole on top. If you have one, place it in a central position on your ornament so it balances perfectly when you hang it.

LEGO® Technic axle connector holds the string

FELIX FELICIS

It may look like a wintry icicle, but this is actually a vial of Felix Felicis—a powerful good luck potion. Don't worry if it falls off the tree. Your luck won't run out.

A bar with stopper runs through this 2×2 transparent round brick

FLYING CAR

Who needs Santa's sleigh when you have a flying Ford Anglia? Mr. Weasley's car looks better hanging from a Christmas tree than hanging from a Whomping Willow.

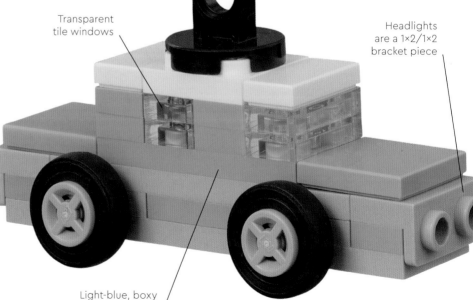

Transparent tile windows

Headlights are a 1×2/1×2 bracket piece

Teardrop-shaped vial

Light-blue, boxy bodywork

NEXT STOP, CHRISTMAS

All aboard the Christmas tree! Red is one of the traditional colors of Christmas, and it also happens to be the color of the Hogwarts Express. Build this mini train to combine Hogwarts wizardry with the magic of Christmas.

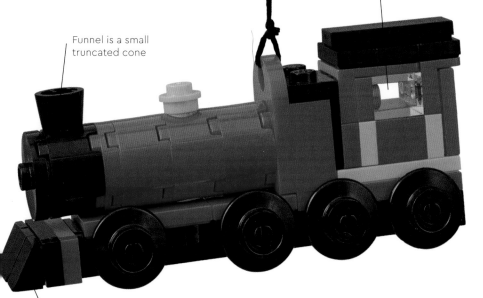

Funnel is a small truncated cone

Sideways 1×2 brick window

Three small slopes make the buffers

Stacked 2×2 round bricks

2×3 curved plate with hole

The engine rests on smooth tiles

HIDDEN HOLE

The train hangs on string that passes through the hole on a red 2×3 curved plate. The piece is built sideways into the middle of the engine and blends in seamlessly with the rest of the train.

BUCKBEAK BAUBLE

Half eagle, half horse... that's Buckbeak the Hippogriff. He'll dangle decoratively from a branch of your tree, looking like he's in mid-flight.

THIS IS WEASLEY THE BEST TREE EVER!

Pyramid slope beak

Feathered wings flap on plates with clips

Mechanical claw pieces are clawed feet

HOGWARTS BOOKENDS

Keep spell books and other tomes tidy with some Hogwarts bookends. These bookends are two halves of Hogwarts castle, with a Dementor on one side and a Quidditch pitch on the other, but pick any theme you like. How about two Diagon Alley shops or the engine and caboose of the Hogwarts Express?

BUILD TIP

Keep your bookends small and wide so they don't topple when tall books are stored inside them. Also keep the backs flat so books can easily slide in and out.

Three different-sized cones form the tallest spire

A microscale dementor circles the school

BASE LAYER

The adjustable base fits into a two-plate-tall gap beneath each of the book ends. It's made from one layer of plates and another layer of tiles, with one 2×2 plate at either end to hold the bookends in position.

This gap is the same width and height as the base

2×2 plate

A LONG, LONG READ

LEGO bookends aren't heavy, so connect them to a base to stop them sliding apart. It's easy to expand your base as your book collection grows. You never know, wizard Gilderoy Lockhart might gift your minifigures a copy of his bestselling autobiography, *Magical Me*.

Slopes and small round tiles for the jagged rocks

BOOKSHELF VIEW

Dementor wings are minifigure flippers

Tall arch marks this out as the clock tower

Open studs are tiny windows

CLOCK TOWER VIEW

Build towers upon towers for magical Hogwarts architecture

PITCH VIEW

Green plates are neatly mowed lawns

Use matching roof tiles for a coherent look

Textured bricks add more realism

Quidditch towers are stacked 1×1 plates topped with tiles

USE THIS TO STORE YOUR SIGNED COPY OF MY BESTSELLING BOOK, HARRY!

BOOK NOOK

Build a Hogwarts-themed book nook to nestle between books on a shelf. This one has Harry in his dormitory and Professor McGonagall in the Great Hall downstairs. She might be checking for Boggarts before bedtime! What will be in your book nook? How about Hermione in the Owlery while a troll rages in the dungeon below?

BUILD TIP

If you'd like to change the rooms in your book nook regularly, make it a modular build so it's easy to take apart and play with. You could even have several stories.

SMALL WORLD

A book nook may be small by nature, but this one is packed with little details that create lots of atmosphere. There are cozy lit candles, wooden floorboards, and tiny bits of furniture.

WHAT'S ALL THAT NOISE AT BEDTIME?

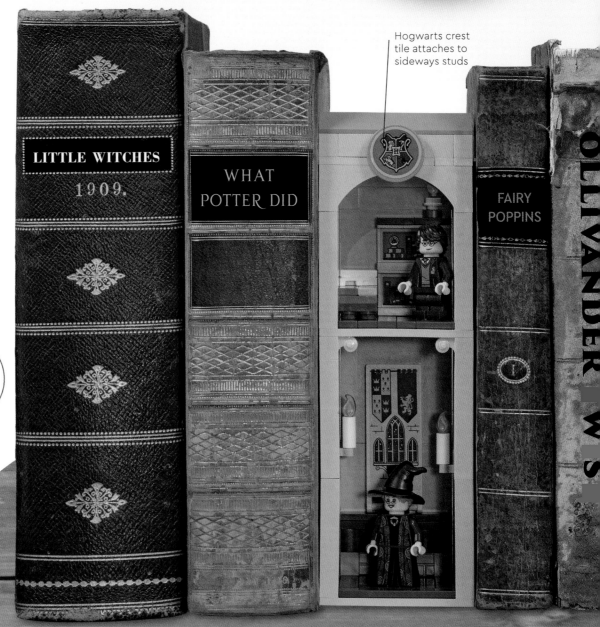

Hogwarts crest tile attaches to sideways studs

MAKE THE BED

Harry's adorable dormitory bed has a 2×4 plate wooden frame with 1×1 round plate legs. Build the checkered blanket by adding 1×1 tiles on top of a second 2×4 plate, and finish with a tile pillow.

2×2 wedge plate for the sheets

1×1 tiles in alternating colors

2×4 plate for the bed base

1×1 round plate

If you don't have arch pieces, make a square ceiling

No stickers? Use small plates for books

HARRY'S DORM

Small brown tiles for a wooden floor

THE WAND IN THE WILLOWS

2×4 double slopes add a hint of the roof

1×6×5 panel pieces fill out the sides

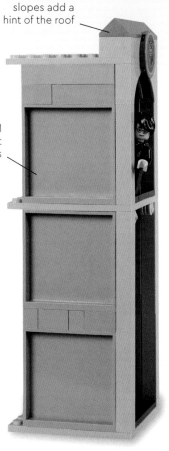

SIDE VIEW

1×1 bricks with scrolls look like ceiling coving

Bricks with clips hold wall candles

Leave exposed studs to pose minifigures on

GREAT HALL

MINIFIGURE DISPLAY CASE

Show off your minifigures in this Hogwarts display case, with places for 14 minifigures (sorry, Voldemort... not you). Perhaps the Dark Lord and his Death Eaters deserve a display case of their own. You could hide it on the reverse of this one! What other buildings or locations can you think of that could make good minifigure display cases?

SIDE VIEW

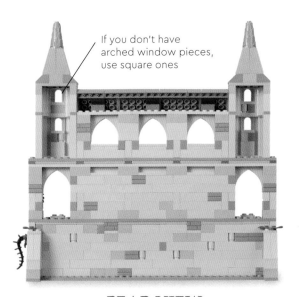

If you don't have arched window pieces, use square ones

REAR VIEW

STANDING PROUD

Include alcoves with little plinths for minifigures to stand on. Add more tiers or build the case wider if you have lots to display. Taller minifigures, like Hagrid, will need extra headroom, so make at least one tier extra-tall.

2×4×3 half cones shape the lower parts of the spires

This tier has more height than the others

SLOPING SET-UP

The long castle roof, made from plates and tiles, attaches to three pairs of hinge bricks and plates so it fits on at a sloping angle.

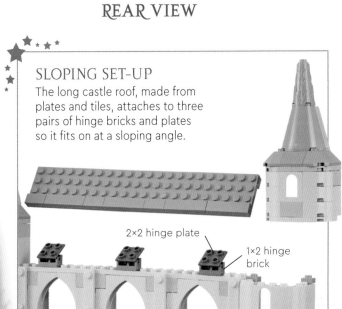

2×2 hinge plate

1×2 hinge brick

ANY ROOM FOR ME?

Each minifigure stands on two 1×2 jumper plates

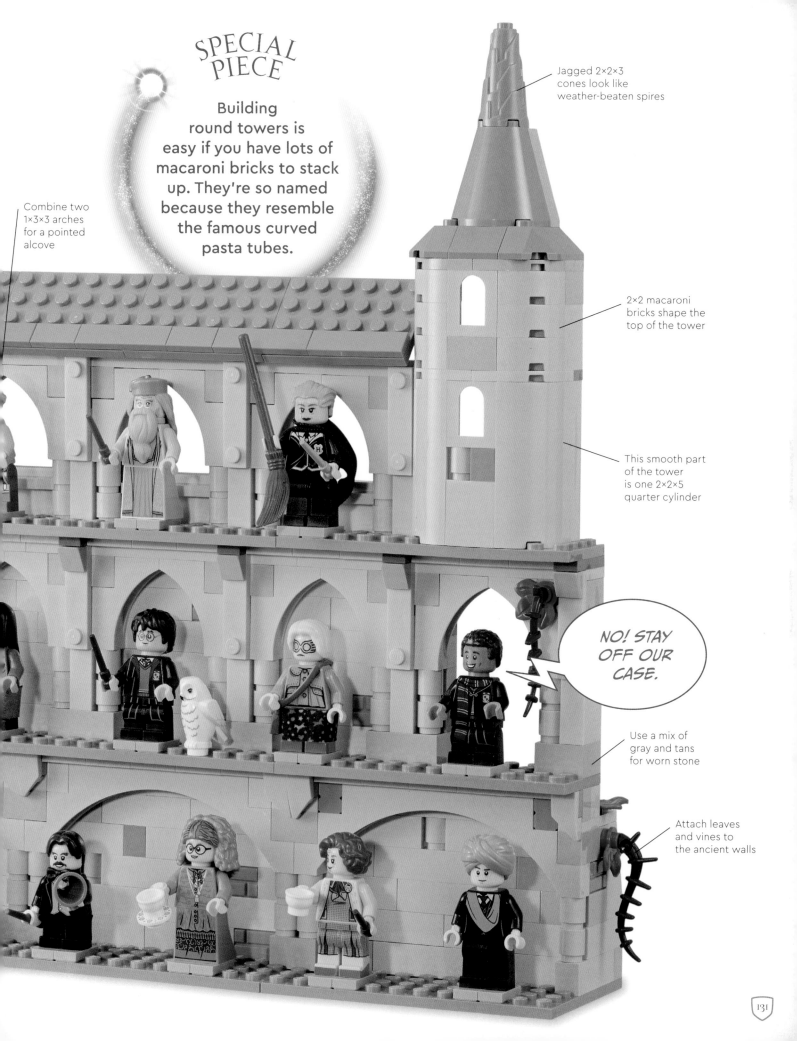

Building round towers is easy if you have lots of macaroni bricks to stack up. They're so named because they resemble the famous curved pasta tubes.

Combine two 1×3×3 arches for a pointed alcove

Jagged 2×2×3 cones look like weather-beaten spires

2×2 macaroni bricks shape the top of the tower

This smooth part of the tower is one 2×2×5 quarter cylinder

NO! STAY OFF OUR CASE.

Use a mix of gray and tans for worn stone

Attach leaves and vines to the ancient walls

WIZARD DESK CADDIES

Unlike in the Harry Potter movies, in real life you can't wave a magic wand and put things away. But you can build these Hogwarts desk caddies to make organizing all your tiny objects more fun. Can you think of any other storage ideas? You could build a coiled serpent pen pot, or how about a cauldron-shaped trinket bowl?

BUILD TIP

To make a removable roof like that on the Hogwarts desk caddy, build a rim of smooth tiles around the top of the compartment it sits on. Include a few exposed studs for the roof to loosely attach to.

Textured spire is a 2×2×3 jagged cone

Minifigure ski poles top the spires

Slope bricks make good roof tiles

1×3 arches shape the stained-glass windows

Place your longest items in this tall tower

THERE'S EVEN A PLACE FOR MY WAND!

1×2×1 panel pieces create interesting wall details

KEEPING STATIONERY

Pens, pencils, erasers, and sticky notes could all go in this Hogwarts Castle stationery holder. Include a secret compartment to hold extra-valuable items.

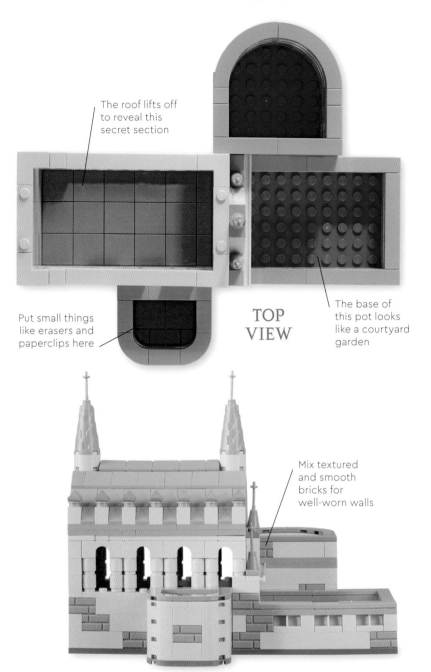

The roof lifts off to reveal this secret section

Put small things like erasers and paperclips here

TOP VIEW

The base of this pot looks like a courtyard garden

PINNACLE OF PERFECTION

This detailed roof build has a hidden base of rows of 1×8 bricks. They not only provide a stable base for the sloping roof tiles. Leave their ends exposed and they can create little spires called pinnacles, which are a Gothic architectural feature.

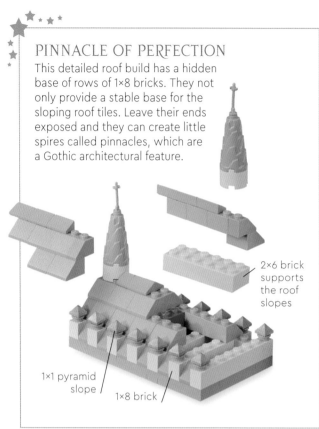

2×6 brick supports the roof slopes

1×1 pyramid slope

1×8 brick

Mix textured and smooth bricks for well-worn walls

SIDE VIEW

2×2 round jumper plate for iris

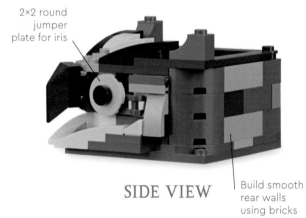

SIDE VIEW

Build smooth rear walls using bricks

HOOT FOR LOOT

This big-eyed owl pot can be used to store jewelry, trinkets, tiny toys, or other small things like earbuds. You could even make a Hedwig or Errol pot. If owls don't get your imagination flying, try a cat, a rat, or a wide-mouthed toad.

1×6 tiles make a smooth rim

Ear tufts are 1×2 inverted arches

Small tiles line the inside

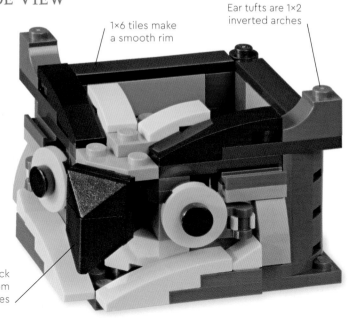

Hooked black beak made from two slope pieces

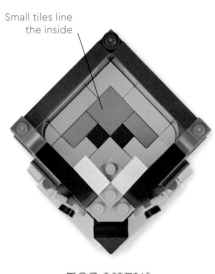

TOP VIEW

133

MAGICAL NEWSPAPER

The Daily Prophet is not for sale at real-world newsstands, but don't despair. This LEGO version of the wizarding newspaper allows you to write your own magical headlines and build your own moving photos. What's this week's big scoop?

SPECIAL PIECES

The newspaper's headlines are created from letter-printed 1×1 round tiles found in LEGO® Dots sets. They're available in every letter of the alphabet.

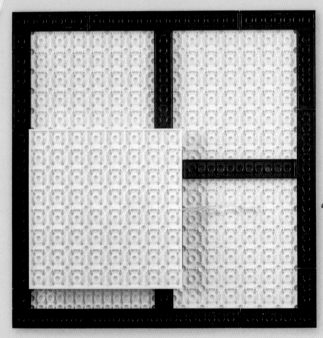

REAR VIEW

HOLD THE FRONT PAGE!

READ ALL ABOUT IT!

Your headline article should be the most attention-grabbing news of the week. This one reports on a mysterious flying car that has caused shock and awe in the Muggle world. Save the gossip or scandal for your secondary story.

FORD ANGLIA IN FLIGHT

The flying car picture is built on a separate plate that attaches via bricks to the newspaper text. Leave a gap at one side of the picture so you can poke through the car, which sits on a transparent bar. Hold the other end to make the car fly!

This side of the plate is left open

1×12 transparent bar with 1×2 plate and 1×1 round stud

The rest of the picture is built on this level

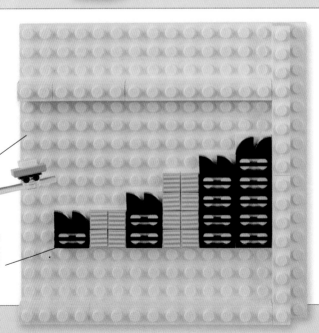

SIDE VIEW

The first letter of an article is often the biggest

Use plain 1×1 round tiles for spaces or leave exposed studs

The newspaper's name has a fancy design around it

THE
DAILY PROPHET
FLYING FORD ANGLIA
MYSTIFIES MUGGLES

CK TO LOC
LO   K
F
H
A
R
T SIGN
ING

Narrow tiles represent smaller text in the article

A magical newspaper's headlines don't have to print in a straight line

1×2 grille tiles and striped 1×1 tiles look like city skyscrapers

HOLD ON... THAT'S MY CAR!

CREATE YOUR CREST

Take inspiration from the Hogwarts crest and design a cool one for a different school using colorful LEGO pieces. How about a school for LEGO builders, a sports or art school, or a school for wizarding folk who can't get into Hogwarts? You could even build your own school's crest.

Rounded corners are 1×2×1⅓ curved slopes

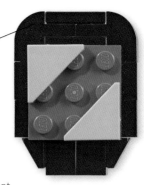

White plates here make the black initial stand out

How many different crest shapes can you create?

HOUSE COLORS

Be inspired by this Hogwarts crest, which has the school's bold, high-contrast house colors built onto a background shape created by slope bricks. An "H" for Hogwarts is set right in the middle.

1×2×3 slope brick side

CRESTS

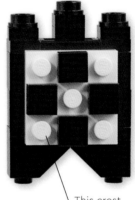

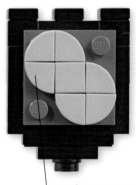

1×2 inverted slope bricks shape the bottom

HOGWARTS CREST

This crest would work for a chess club

Mostly 1×1 quarter tiles create this shape

HOUSEKEEPING

Each house color on the Hogwarts crest is represented by one or two plates, which attach to bricks with side studs built into the curved background shape.

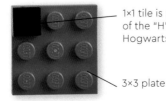

1×1 tile is part of the "H" for Hogwarts

1×2 brick with two side studs

3×3 plate

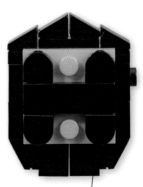

Spell out initials with tiles

Heart tiles make this crest look welcoming

CRESTS AND BANNERS

As well as school crests, you could design family crests for you and your friends. Try making some school banners or flags, too, ready to hang proudly at home.

Alternate colors for a checkerboard effect

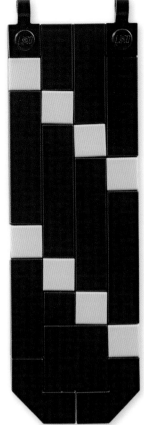

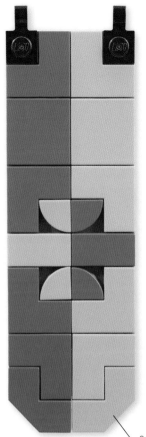

2×2 corner tiles with cutouts make an angular shape

BANNERS

These banners hang from 1×1 plates with clips

Small, swirling tiles look like a slithering snake

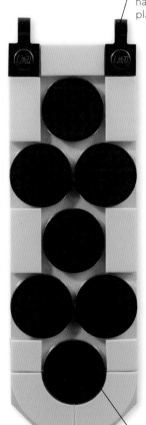

Each banner has a bottom layer of plates

I DEMAND THAT YOU MAKE A MALFOY CREST!

Play with tile shapes and colors

FESTIVE SWEATERS

Every Christmas, Mrs. Weasley knits festive sweaters as gifts. They're ideal for magical folk and Muggles alike... even Harry's cocky cousin, Dudley. You won't need knitting needles to make these sweaters—just LEGO pieces. Put the recipient's initial on the front, add their lucky number, or even create a portrait of them.

BUILD TIP

If you build a large collection of sweaters, like this one, build curved hangers onto their necks using brown, black, or gray pieces for easy storage!

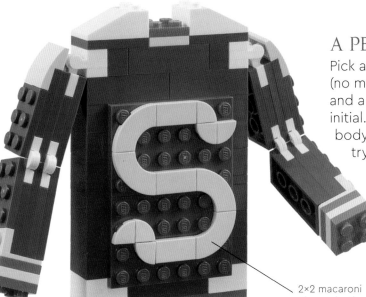

A PERFECT FIT

Pick a color your giftee loves (no maroon for Ron, thank you) and a contrasting hue for the initial. Stripes add detail to the body and cuffs, or you could try a checkered or spotted pattern instead. These sweaters are all posable, thanks to jointed elbows and shoulders.

2×2 macaroni tiles make the curves of this "S"

Striped cuff made from 2×2 plates

SIDE VIEW

KNITTICUS WOOLICUS.

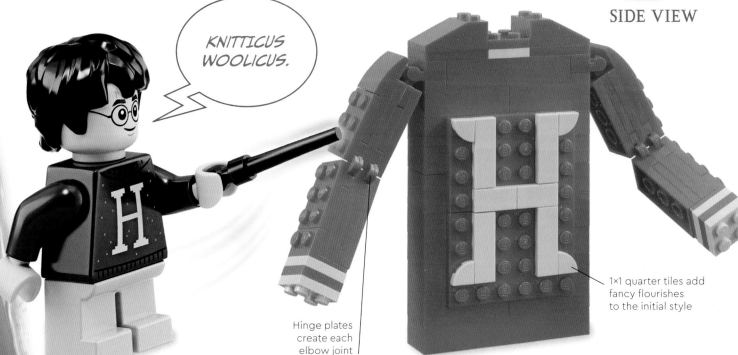

Hinge plates create each elbow joint

1×1 quarter tiles add fancy flourishes to the initial style

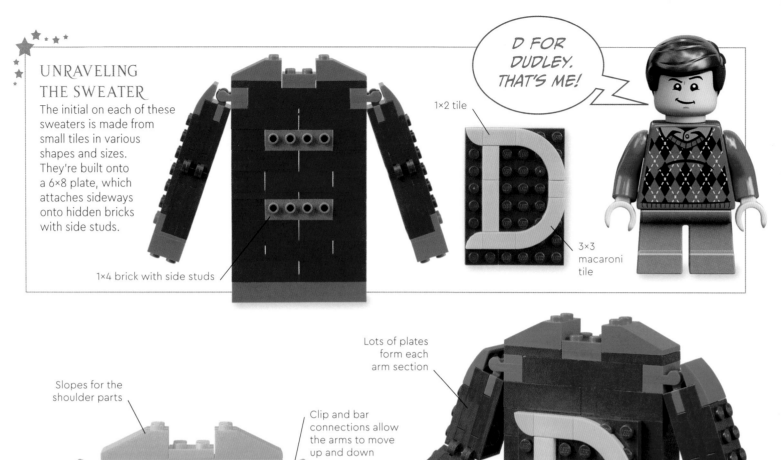

UNRAVELING THE SWEATER

The initial on each of these sweaters is made from small tiles in various shapes and sizes. They're built onto a 6×8 plate, which attaches sideways onto hidden bricks with side studs.

1×4 brick with side studs

D FOR DUDLEY. THAT'S ME!

1×2 tile

3×3 macaroni tile

Slopes for the shoulder parts

Clip and bar connections allow the arms to move up and down

Lots of plates form each arm section

Alternate brick colors for a wide-striped sweater

Make the hem a different color for extra detail

1×2/2×2 angle plates here let the cuffs attach sideways

STATION SIGNS

There's no need to visit Kings Cross station in London. Build these train signs and the magic of the Hogwarts Express will come right to you. The signs make great decorations to prop up on a shelf or hang from a wall or door in your home.

BUILD TIP

Build little stands at the back of your signs so they're freestanding, like these. Or attach plates with holes to allow them to hang from your walls.

SIDEWAYS SIGN

Each letter in the Hogwarts Express sign is built sideways, like this "H." Tan plates and bricks form the letters, and dark-red plates and bricks fill in the gaps between the letters.

Tiles and plates create the sign's sides

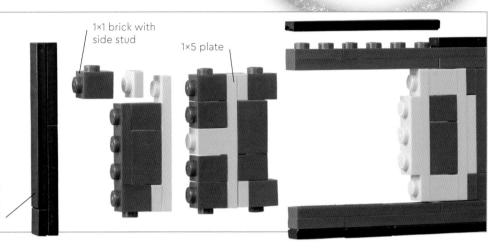

1×1 brick with side stud

1×5 plate

SPELL IT OUT

Create your own eye-catching Hogwarts Express lettering, for use on the side of a train or a platform sign. (Well, we don't want Hogwarts students accidentally boarding the 8:25 to Aberdeen!) Slopes at the back of the model keep it upright.

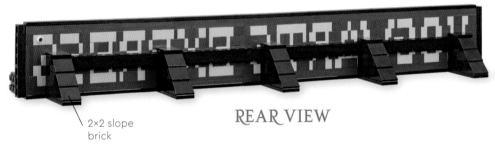

2×2 slope brick

REAR VIEW

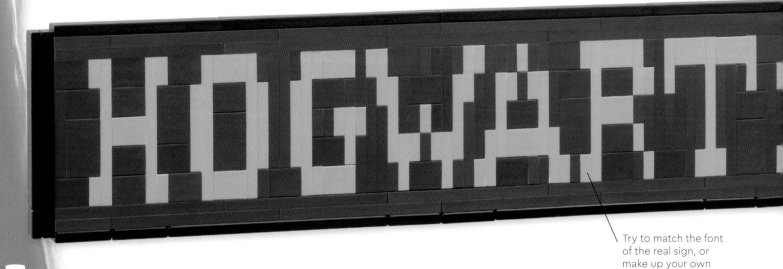

Try to match the font of the real sign, or make up your own

MAGICAL PLATFORM

Hogwarts students run through a brick wall to reach platform 9¾ at the station. Don't copy them and try running at this LEGO platform sign. You might just have to build your model all over again.

Small black tiles create the numbers

The "round" tan part is made from eight square and rectangular plates

2×16 plate stand leg

2×4 hinge plates connect the sign to the stand legs

REAR VIEW

Outline the sign in the burgundy of the Hogwarts Express

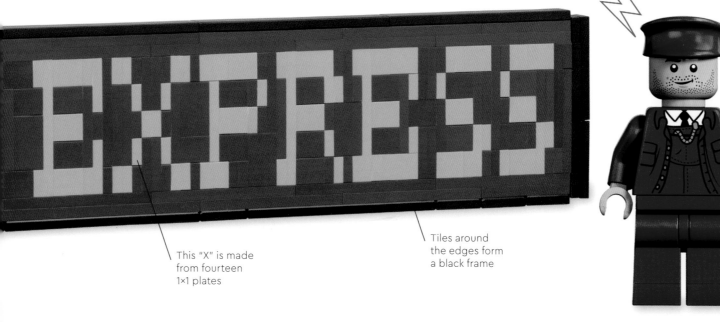

This "X" is made from fourteen 1×1 plates

Tiles around the edges form a black frame

TICKETS, PLEASE! WE ALSO ACCEPT BRICKETS.

141

CHAPTER FOUR

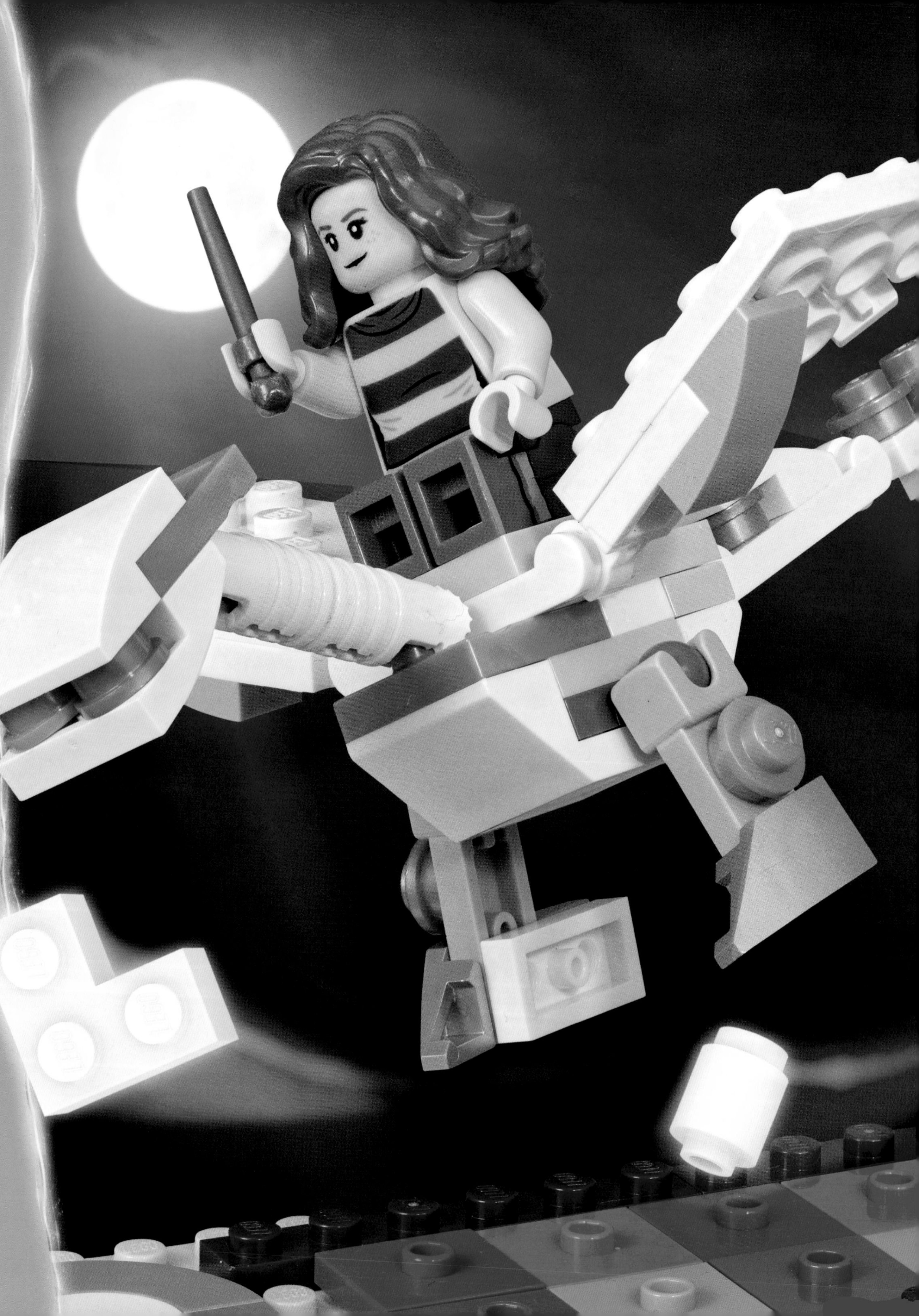

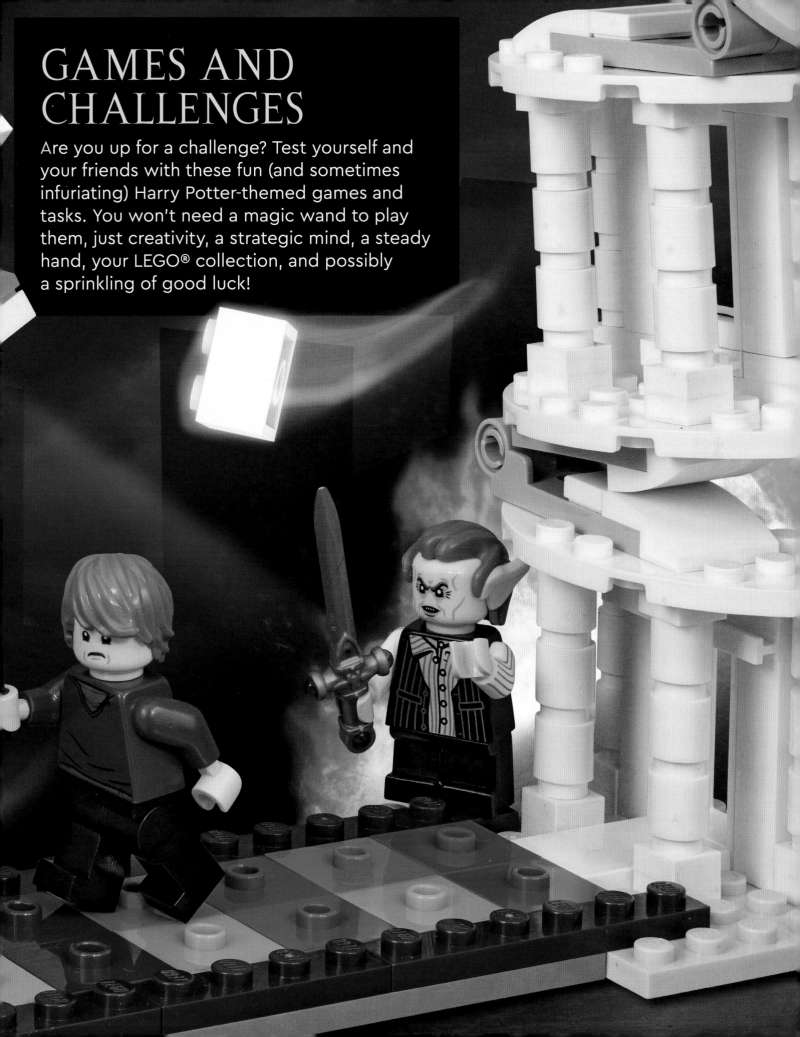

GAMES AND CHALLENGES

Are you up for a challenge? Test yourself and your friends with these fun (and sometimes infuriating) Harry Potter-themed games and tasks. You won't need a magic wand to play them, just creativity, a strategic mind, a steady hand, your LEGO® collection, and possibly a sprinkling of good luck!

TRIWIZARD DRAGON CHALLENGE

The Triwizard Cup is a thrilling three-part contest between three schools of magic. Now is your chance to enter a LEGO® version! In this first trial, a golden egg is up for grabs. Will your minifigure get to it before their dragon attacks? It's time to find out, so get cracking.

COURAGEOUS CONTESTANTS

This game is for two to four players, represented by a Harry Potter, Viktor Krum, Fleur Delacour, or Cedric Diggory minifigure. Who will be the first to reach the golden egg while avoiding an attack from their dragon?

Each counter must be the same size

COUNTERS

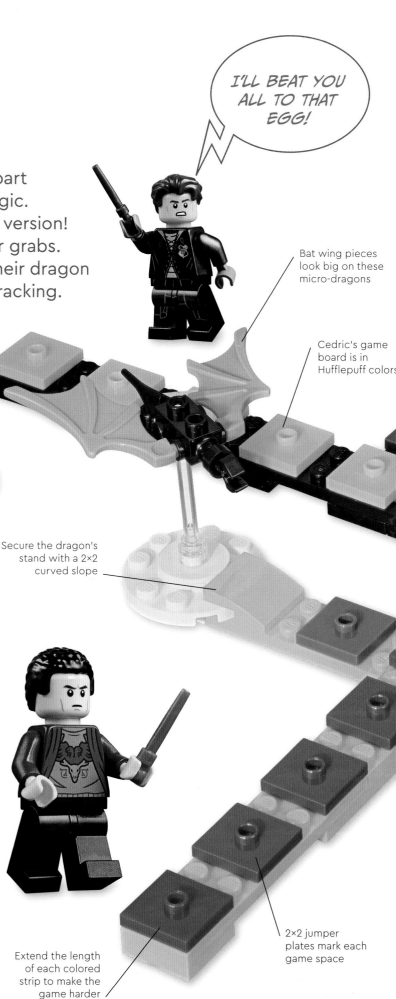

I'LL BEAT YOU ALL TO THAT EGG!

Bat wing pieces look big on these micro-dragons

Cedric's game board is in Hufflepuff colors

Secure the dragon's stand with a 2×2 curved slope

2×2 jumper plates mark each game space

Extend the length of each colored strip to make the game harder

HOW TO PLAY

1 Place one purple, two red, and three green tile counters in a bag. Players take turns drawing one from the bag. A green tile means their minifigure moves forward one space. A red tile means it stands still. A purple tile means their dragon moves forward one space.

2 If a player's dragon gets to the egg before their minifigure, the dragon turns on the minifigure and chases it back to the beginning.

3 The winner is the player whose minifigure reaches the egg first.

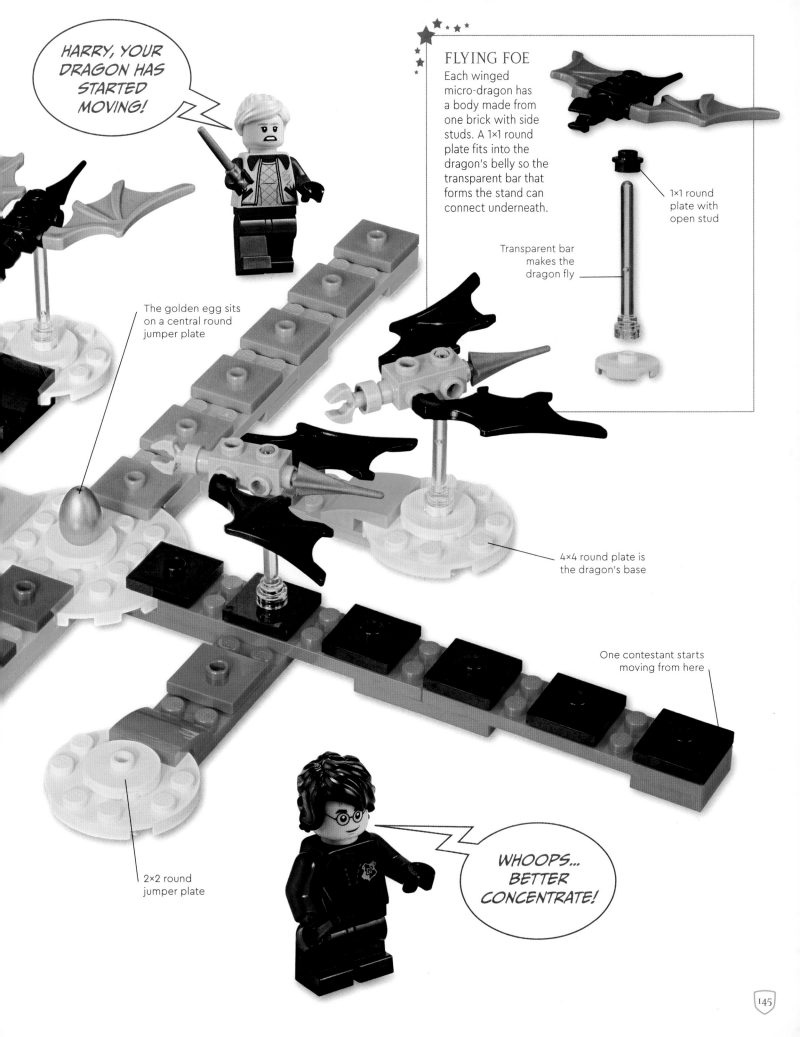

HARRY, YOUR DRAGON HAS STARTED MOVING!

FLYING FOE

Each winged micro-dragon has a body made from one brick with side studs. A 1×1 round plate fits into the dragon's belly so the transparent bar that forms the stand can connect underneath.

1×1 round plate with open stud

Transparent bar makes the dragon fly

The golden egg sits on a central round jumper plate

4×4 round plate is the dragon's base

One contestant starts moving from here

2×2 round jumper plate

WHOOPS... BETTER CONCENTRATE!

TRIWIZARD UNDERWATER CHALLENGE

The second task in the Triwizard Tournament is a watery one. Race a rival to free a minifigure classmate who is chained up underwater, shoving aside algae and seagrass as you go. First to the rescue wins the game... and maybe gets a squelchy hug from their soggy schoolmate. Yuk!

HOW TO PLAY

1 The two players choose their favorite Triwizard contestant minifigure to play: Fleur Delacour, Viktor Krum, Cedric Diggory, or Harry Potter.

2 Players take turns to roll a die and move along the course. Player 1 must roll a four or above to move forward one space. Player 2 must roll a three or below.

3 Every time a player moves forward, they must push a water plant aside. The winner is the first player to make it to the chained-up minifigure.

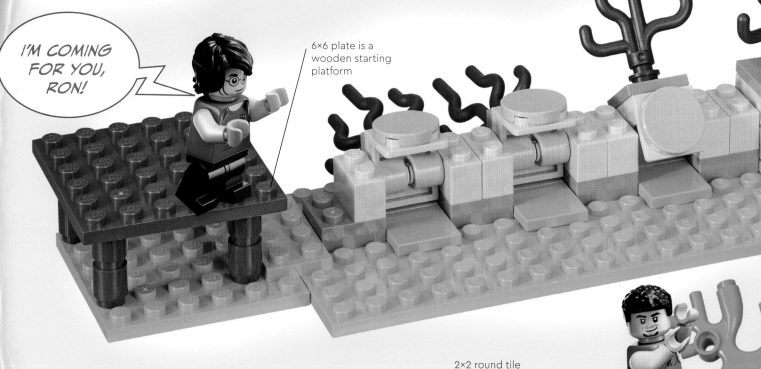

I'M COMING FOR YOU, RON!

6×6 plate is a wooden starting platform

2×2 round tile looks like a stepping stone

IT'S A PUSHOVER

Any plantlike green LEGO pieces can be used for the seagrass and algae. Push them aside and a small platform flips up for the minifigure to stand on. This build uses round tiles for the platforms.

Try building seagrass if you don't have this piece

Secure your chain between rocklike slopes

FAST FLIPPER
Each small platform flips around in an instant thanks to a moving pin-and-hole connection. A plate with hole under the sea plant can rotate 90 degrees on the pins either side of it.

2×2/2×2 bracket plate platform base

2×2 plate with hole

1×2 brick with pin

Add lake-floor scenery such as stones and fish

Seaweed piece fits onto a 2×2 jumper plate

Build on a blue base plate for an underwater feel

1×1 transparent round bricks hold up the floating fish and figures

DON'T TAKE A WRONG TURN, KRUM!

TRIWIZARD MAZE

In this a-maze-ing one-player game, roll a ball through the twists and turns of a pitfall-filled maze to get your hands on the Triwizard Cup. Will you emerge triumphant, like Harry? Or will you take a wrong turn and... oh dear! Tilting the board is the secret to getting the ball past the perilous pits. Let's roll!

BUILD TIP

Find a LEGO ball (or marble) of the right size to pass through the maze. The smaller the ball, the more difficult it will be to navigate through the maze.

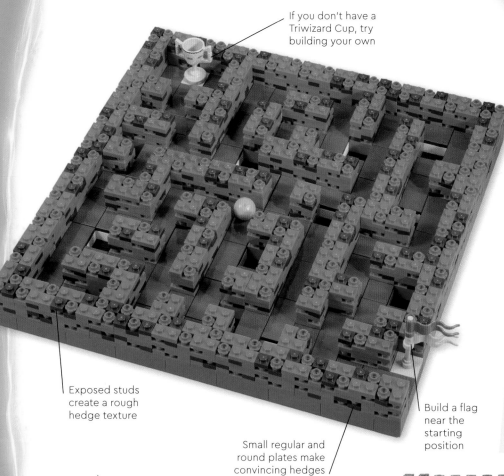

If you don't have a Triwizard Cup, try building your own

Exposed studs create a rough hedge texture

Small regular and round plates make convincing hedges

Build a flag near the starting position

PICK YOUR PITS

Change the number of pits and their placement to make the game easier or harder. Remember, though, some must always be possible to roll past. Winding green hedges confuse the eye but also keep the ball on course.

HOW TO PLAY

1 Place your ball at the start point. Then hold the maze in both hands and begin tilting it this way and that to guide the ball through the twists and turns.

2 If you get the ball to the Triwizard Cup, you win. If it drops into a pit, you'll have to start again.

PLOT IT OUT

To build your own maze, plan out your pathways using white bricks (or any colors you have) and your hedges with green bricks. Then top the white bricks with brown tiles and build up your hedges in between.

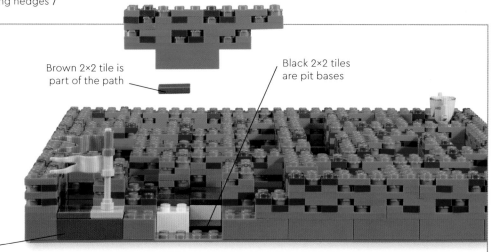

Brown 2×2 tile is part of the path

Black 2×2 tiles are pit bases

This brown brick helps mark the start of the maze

TOP VIEW

Pits are almost one-brick deep

2×2 jumper plate holds the cup

Mix dark and lighter greens for natural foliage

LEGO® Technic ball

LEGO® BIONICLE® sphere

BALL TYPES

LET'S GET THE BALL ROLLING!

TABLETOP QUIDDITCH

Be your own Quidditch team in this tabletop challenge. Build three pieces of equipment and mount your minifigures on their broomsticks, then let the game begin. Can you score with the Quaffle, bat the Bludger, and grab the Golden Snitch before it hits the table? If you can, the only thing left to do is build yourself a winner's trophy.

HOW TO PLAY

1 Start your game by shooting the red Quaffle through the hoops. You must score once in each hoop before you can move on.

2 Grab a Beater's bat and place the black Bludger on its plinth. Take aim at the Beater minifigure in order to knock them over with the Bludger.

3 Next, using the lever, fire the Golden Snitch up through the tower and try to catch it. When you catch the Snitch, you win the game.

BAT THE BLUDGER

Build a mini tower in Hogwarts colors and place the Bludger ball on top of it. Then create a brick-built bat to whack the Bludger with. It might take a few tries to knock the Beater off their perch!

The minifigure's leg fits onto a stud at the end of the stand

YOU'LL NEVER KNOCK ME OVER!

2×2×2 cone shapes this tapering part

Two 1×1 round bricks are the handle

Bludger balances on a 1×1 tile and 1×1 cone plinth

Transparent pieces make the Beater minifigure appear to fly

This 2×2 jumper plate has a stud at its center

Adding a plate here strengthens the tower

BLUDGER STAND

Plain minifigure head

LEGO Technic ball

1×1 round plate

QUIDDITCH CHEST

QUAFFLE   BLUDGER   GOLDEN SNITCH

THROUGH THE HOOPS

To shoot the red Quaffle from the end of the player's broomstick, swoop the minifigure down then flick the ball off the handle and through a hoop using your thumb.

1×8 hoop stand

Sturdy plate bases suggest the Quidditch lawn

Connected 1×3 plates create the hoops

I'M HOOPING TO GET A GOOD SCORE!

GOAL HOOPS

Quaffle fits onto the end of the broom

Snitch shoots out of an opening here

SNATCH THAT SNITCH!

Set the Golden Snitch in the base of the large tower. Press the lever and watch for the Snitch to shoot out of the top. Sometimes the Snitch may not make it out of the tower, but if it does, be quick, as it could go in any direction.

Decorate with Hogwarts crests if you have some

SNITCH LAUNCHER

2×8 plate for the lever

LEVERLAUNCHER

The lever works like a catapult, swiveling on pin pieces in the middle. When the 2×2 round tile at one end is pressed, the other end flips up, launching the Snitch.

This 1×2 slope keeps the Snitch in position

LEGO Technic pin fits through pieces with holes

151

PICK A POTION

Race to mix a potion in this lucky dip game. Will you be first to grab all the ingredients you need, or will a friend beat you to the potion? You'll need a bagful of ingredients, a handful of bonus and pitfall pieces, and some potion recipes to follow. Get picking!

HOW TO PLAY

1 Write down different potion recipes on pieces of paper. Fold them and mix them up.

2 Choose LEGO pieces to represent each ingredient. Then choose one piece for "pick two," one for "lose a turn," and one for "steal an ingredient."

3 Put the LEGO pieces into a bag (or cauldron). Players each choose, unfold, and read a potion recipe.

4 Playing in rounds, players pick pieces out of the bag, gathering ingredients for their potion as they go. If they pull out a "steal" piece, they can take an ingredient from someone who's already picked it.

5 The first player to collect all their potion ingredients is the winner.

BOOM BERRIES

SNAKE

DRAGON FANG

BONE

GOLD

CRYSTAL

COWBANE ESSENCE

CASTOR OIL

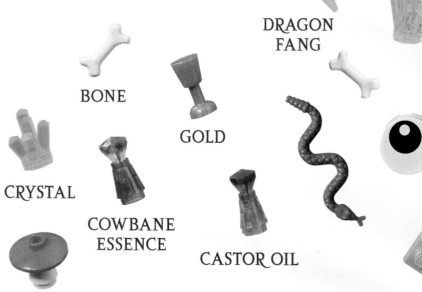

DON'T THINK ABOUT MIXING THOSE INGREDIENTS, SEAMUS!

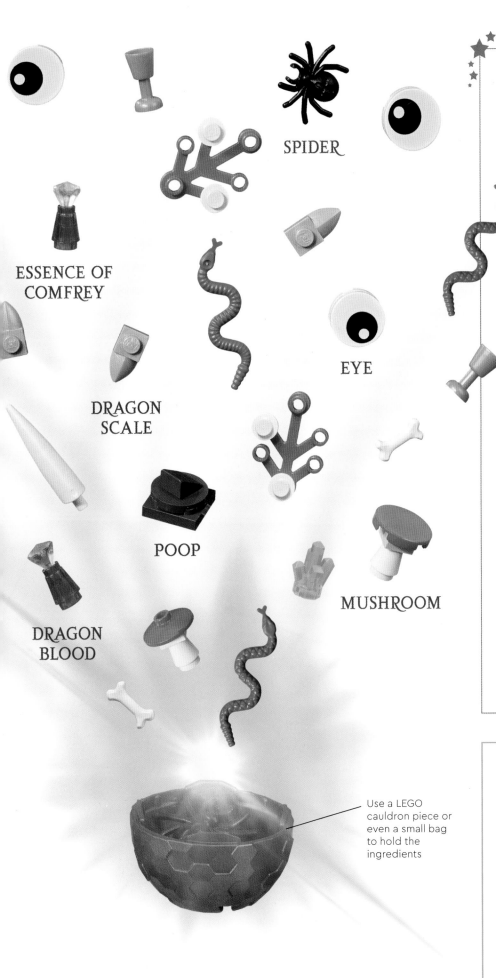

SPIDER

ESSENCE OF
COMFREY

DRAGON
SCALE

EYE

POOP

MUSHROOM

DRAGON
BLOOD

Use a LEGO cauldron piece or even a small bag to hold the ingredients

POTION RECIPES

Make up your own potion recipes or use these ingredients lists for wizarding inspiration. For fairness, make sure all of your potion recipes have the same number of ingredients.

LOVE POTION
2 X BOOM BERRIES
1 X DRAGON SCALE
1 X COWBANE ESSENCE
1 X MUSHROOM

SUPER POISON
1 X GREEN SNAKE
2 X DRAGON FANG
1 X BONE
1 X EYE

ELIXIR OF CONFUSION
1 X BOOM BERRIES
1 X DRAGON SCALE
1 X ESSENCE OF COMFREY
2 X MUSHROOMS

STRENGTH POTION
1 X GOLD
2 X BONE
1 X EYE
1 X DRAGON SCALE

 STEAL AN INGREDIENT

 PICK TWO INGREDIENTS

 LOSE A TURN

153

DEMENTOR BOWLING

Harry Potter used a Patronus to knock out a swarm of soul-sucking Dementors. In this LEGO bowling game, you must try to do the same. Arrange your dark and doomy Dementors in rows, then roll a luminous Patronus at them to knock them over. How many can you take down in one try? Ready... aim... bowl!

BUILD TIP

Build as many Dementors as you like for this game. If you don't have enough black pieces, mix in gray, brown, or white ones to create an equally gloomy effect.

SECRET SQUARE

There's a core of white bricks with side studs hidden inside the Patronus. Attach transparent blue plates on all sides to form the Patronus's glowing body.

1×2×1⅓ brick with side studs

1×2 plate

THAT'S ONE DEMENTOR FEWER!

GOOD HIT, HARRY!

Two 1×1 slopes are the small snout

LET IT ROLL

A Patronus always takes the form of an animal, so it won't be an exact ball shape. However, it must be roundish for this game so it will roll. This Patronus is based on Harry's, which is a deer. What shape will yours be?

Little 1×1 round plates for legs keep the body shape rollable

Layered wedge plates create a jagged cloak

Small, anonymous head made from 2×2 dome pieces

BOWLED OVER

The shadowy Dementors' black cloaks hang over tall stands so they appear to be floating. Make the base of each stand quite narrow—if the pins are too stable, you'll never knock them over!

Stacked round bricks form the tall stand

4×4 round plate base

Aim the Patronus at the pins' bases

PATRONUS IN PLAY

HIDDEN AXLE

Connect each Dementor's body and base builds together using a long cross axle piece. The axle can be threaded through bricks and plates with axle holes built into the two sections.

This 2×2 brick with grooves has an axle hole

LEGO Technic cross axle

HOW TO PLAY

1 Stand the Dementor pins at the end of a table or on the floor. If you have a lot, arrange them in rows, with the widest row at the back.

2 Players take turns to bowl the Patronus at the Dementors. They score one point for every Dementor they knock over. If a player knocks them all over in one strike, they score an extra five points.

3 Play in rounds, writing down everyone's scores. The top scorer at the end of six rounds is the winner.

TOWER OF TREATS

For some feast-time fun in the Great Hall, try this dessert-stacking game. It's less messy than a food fight! Stack the LEGO cakes and pastries higher and higher on the table, but be careful... the stack will become increasingly wobbly as you go. And don't get tempted to taste the treats as you stack. They may look delicious, but they're not edible!

HOW TO PLAY

1 Choose a Hogwarts student or teacher to represent you in the game and seat their minifigure at the banquet table.

2 Players takes turns to stack one treat at a time, forming a tower on the tabletop. You can only attach each treat by two studs, so skill will be needed to keep the tower balanced.

3 The player who topples the tower is the loser and receives an imaginary wooden spoon. Or you can build one!

CAKES AND PASTRIES

This radar dish is printed with sprinkles

Stacked plates are layers of cake and cream

Just two pieces create this flan

If you don't have lots of plates, use bricks instead

1×1 round plates with petals are piped icing

OH CRUMBS... THAT STACK IS GETTING WOBBLY!

FANCY A SLICE?

This wedge of cake is built from two curved pieces that fit snugly inside each other. A 1×1 headlight brick in the corner provides one stud on top and one at the side for stacking.

1×3×2 curved arch

1×2×1⅓ curved slope

1×1 headlight brick

4×4 round plates make this bigger cake

WOBBLY STACK

This game is tricker if you build desserts in different shapes and sizes. To add even more variety, include other feast items like pizzas and chocolate bars. Use pieces with exposed studs because the treats must attach to each other and to the table.

This tower is zigzagging across the table

BUILD TIP

The fewer exposed studs a dessert build has, the trickier it will be to stack. The cake with sprinkles at the top here only has one exposed stud. Good luck to the next player!

THIS GAME IS NOT A PIECE OF CAKE!

Treats must attach by just two studs

Large cakes may topple more easily

Which unlucky player will topple the tower of treats?

This treat is ready to stack

Long table has a top of two 6×8 plates

Build a bench for minifigure players to sit on

BANQUET TABLE

DECK THE HALL

Challenge yourself to organize this year's Christmas decorations at Hogwarts. Fill the Great Hall with festive flourishes, then think about some other scenes. How would the Weasleys do it down at The Burrow? Where would Hagrid put holly in his hut? Try decorating a LEGO room for another event, such as the Hogwarts Halloween feast, too.

BUILD TIP

The colors you build with play an important role in creating an atmosphere. This small build has a Hogwarts feel thanks to dark-red and brown hues.

Build brick wall panels if you don't have these screens

JOLLY HOLLY

Candles, presents, food for feasting, and a cheerful holly wreath create a sparkling scene in the Great Hall. Don't forget a tree with colorful twinkle lights. The lights here are quite possibly made by real fairies.

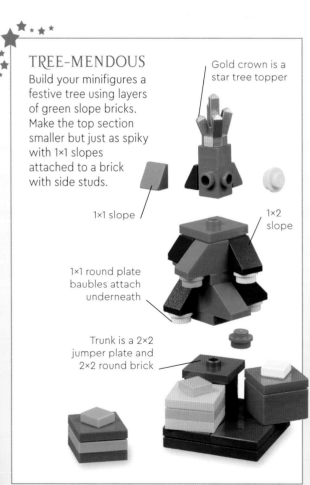

TREE-MENDOUS

Build your minifigures a festive tree using layers of green slope bricks. Make the top section smaller but just as spiky with 1×1 slopes attached to a brick with side studs.

Gold crown is a star tree topper

1×1 slope

1×2 slope

1×1 round plate baubles attach underneath

Trunk is a 2×2 jumper plate and 2×2 round brick

Carrots attach to 1×1 tiles with clips

Include 1×2 jumper plates in the tabletop for attaching items to

TOP VIEW (FEAST TABLE)

You're never far from an owl at Hogwarts

Hand-make a holly wreath from a green lifebuoy and cherry piece

1×4 arch piece tops the fireplace

No Hogwarts-themed stickers? How could you build what's pictured?

Wooden wall panels are 1×2 log bricks

Build minifigure-size presents from just a few pieces

Cream pie—add all your dream feast items

NO PEEKING AT THE PRESENTS, RON!

Twist around 1×1 plates for fancy table legs

159

MAKE A MUGGLE ITEM MAGICAL

This extra-long toast rack resembles the one used at breakfast in Hogwarts Great Hall. Unlike the real thing, it won't float to and from the kitchen, but it looks the part. Make your own long, floating rack and then decide what other household items could use a little magic. How about a self-sweeping broom or walking laundry basket?

CRUMBS, THAT'S A LOT OF TOAST!

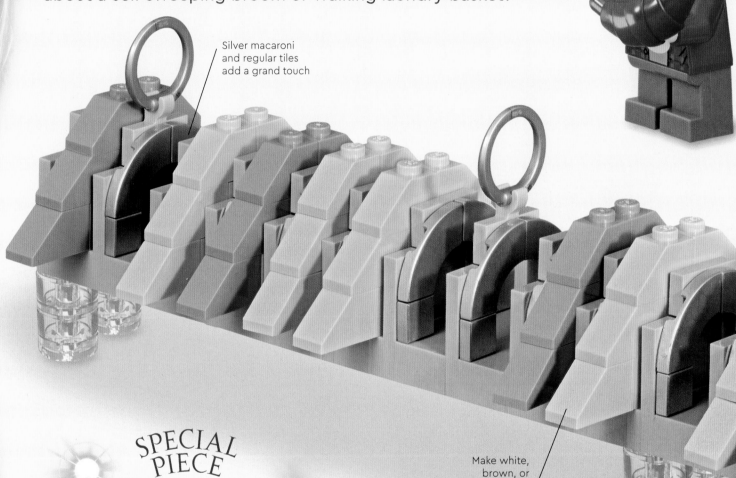

Silver macaroni and regular tiles add a grand touch

Make white, brown, or multigrain toast

SPECIAL PIECE

The flat silver hoops at the top of the toast rack have small, rounded bars at the bottom. This bar allows a clip (or LEGO minifigure hand) to hold onto the element.

A VERY LONG BREAKFAST

How long do you want your toast rack to be? You're only limited by the size of your LEGO collection (and perhaps the length of your dining table). Raise the rack on transparent round bricks so it appears to be floating in mid-air.

WHITE OR BROWN?

You'll want some LEGO toast to slot into your toast rack. Build easy-to-hold half slices, using slope bricks to create smooth crusts. The bad news is this toast can't be eaten, but at least there won't be any crumbs to clean up when you've finished playing!

1×2 slope bricks shape the triangular slices

Darker tan pieces are a well-done crust

Fill the rack with toast or leave spaces where someone has taken a slice

REPETITIVE RACK

Each compartment of the toast rack is built the same way. Bricks and plates lying on their sides attach to upright plates and tiles. Include some bricks with side studs for attaching the stands underneath, and hoops at regular intervals for pulling the rack toward you.

1×2 plate with clip holds up the hoop

1×3 plate

1×4 brick with side studs (pointing down)

2×2 round brick

Upside-down round bricks form transparent stands

2×2 round tiles smooth out the stands' bases

BOGGART CHALLENGE

Boggarts are pesky. They take the form of a person's biggest fear. But don't worry, magical folk can banish them with laughter. In this game, two players take turns to transform each others' Boggart-build fears. One player builds a Boggart, then the second player gets to add something to make the Boggart look funny. A party hat and clown nose? Riddikulus!

WHO'S THERE?

Boggarts lurk in a mysterious cabinet until they burst out to scare the socks off students (or make them giggle). Make your cabinet big enough for some really big fears. If you prefer, build a simpler box or screen.

Add gold pieces for a grand, Hogwarts touch

Sharp 1×1 round plate teeth emerge first

PHEW, IT'S NOT A SPIDER!

6×12 plate is the cabinet door

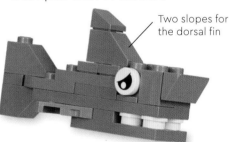

Two slopes for the dorsal fin

SHARK BOGGART

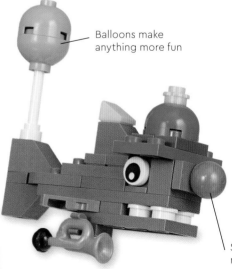

Balloons make anything more fun

Switch the pointy nose for a 1×2 jumper plate and ball piece

CLOWN SHARK

162

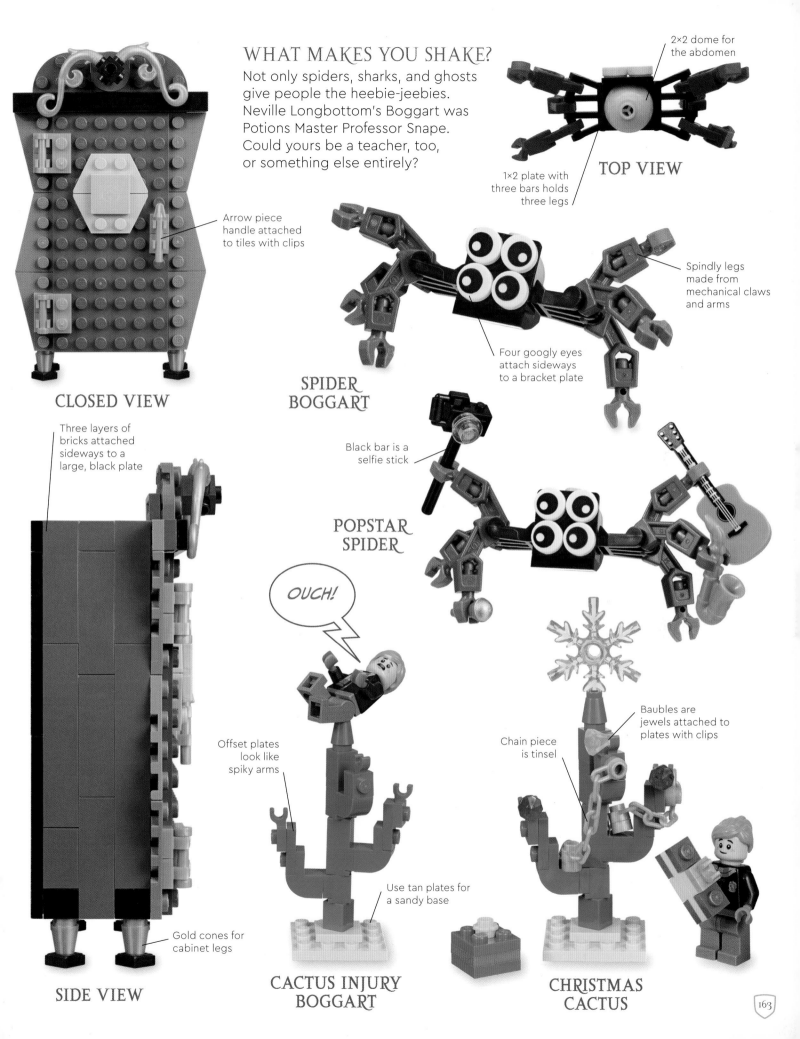

WHAT MAKES YOU SHAKE?

Not only spiders, sharks, and ghosts give people the heebie-jeebies. Neville Longbottom's Boggart was Potions Master Professor Snape. Could yours be a teacher, too, or something else entirely?

2×2 dome for the abdomen

TOP VIEW

1×2 plate with three bars holds three legs

Arrow piece handle attached to tiles with clips

CLOSED VIEW

Spindly legs made from mechanical claws and arms

SPIDER BOGGART

Four googly eyes attach sideways to a bracket plate

Three layers of bricks attached sideways to a large, black plate

Black bar is a selfie stick

POPSTAR SPIDER

OUCH!

Offset plates look like spiky arms

Gold cones for cabinet legs

SIDE VIEW

Use tan plates for a sandy base

CACTUS INJURY BOGGART

Chain piece is tinsel

Baubles are jewels attached to plates with clips

CHRISTMAS CACTUS

163

SORTING HAT SPINNER

Gryffindor, Slytherin, Ravenclaw, or Hufflepuff... which Hogwarts house do you imagine you belong in? Let the Sorting Hat decide in this super spinner game. Remember, no cheating. You can't have a second try if you don't get the house you want (at least not while anyone is watching). The Sorting Hat is never wrong!

A NEW ARRIVAL? GREETINGS

SLITHER OVER TO SLYTHERIN.

Just one 2×2×2 slope brick makes the length of the hat

Overhanging point is two slopes with cutouts

Gold tiles divide the houses

1×1 cone pointer decides your Hogwarts house

Dark-red 6×6 plate represents Gryffindor house

HUFFLEPUFF WOULD BE HAPPY TO HAVE YOU!

GO FOR A SPIN

The base of this build is made of four square plates in the house colors. A round plate forms the brim of the Sorting Hat, which spins on a round brick below. Don't forget a pointer on the brim.

GRYFFINDOR

If you are put into Gryffindor, the Sorting Hat must think you are brave, adventurous, and noble. Congratulations! Harry, Ron, and Hermione might be your friends, and you could meet the house ghost, Nearly Headless Nick.

SLYTHERIN

The Sorting Hat will put you in Slytherin if you are ambitious and cunning. Don't be put off by this house's shady reputation. Just think, you could have Draco Malfoy as a best friend, and you might learn to talk to snakes. Sssssssplendid!

HUFFLEPUFF

Are you honest, hardworking, and loyal? That's why the Sorting Hat has put you in Hufflepuff. You're probably popular, too, like famous Triwizard champion Cedric Diggory. Who doesn't love someone they can trust?

RAVENCLAW

Straight As to you if the Sorting Hat puts you in Ravenclaw. Only the brainiest students get into this high-flying house. But keep studying, because Luna Lovegood and Cho Chang may be going all out to beat you in exams.

COME INSIDE, BRAINIACS!

A hidden axle pin connects the cone here

4×4 macaroni tiles line the rim

Decorate the corners with more gold tiles because... why not?

SIDE VIEW

GET TO THE POINT

There's LEGO magic going on below the rim of the Sorting Hat. A discreet 4×4 round brick spins on a pin to make the hat turn, while the pointer fits neatly next to the round brick on the underside of the brim.

This 2×2 plate has a pin hole on the bottom

8×8 round plate hat base

4×4 round brick with hole

2×2 tile with pin

CHARADES

Gather a bunch of friends and give this Harry Potter charades game a whirl! Spin the carousel in the tower, then silently act out the minifigure who appears in the window. If you're good, the other players will guess who the character is. If not... well, maybe you can inquire about drama classes.

HOW TO PLAY

1 Players take turns to be the spinner, who spins the carousel with the tower facing toward them. They must close their eyes so they don't see all the characters as the carousel spins.

2 When the carousel stops, the spinner must silently act out the character they can see through the open window. Other players must not see the minifigure.

3 If the other players guess the spinner's character correctly within two minutes, the spinner gets one point.

4 If a minifigure is guessed correctly, take it off the carousel and replace it with another. The winning player is the one with the most points at the end of the game.

2×2×2 slope bricks form the roof

The towers around the edges are static

WOOHOO! MY TURN AT LAST.

Slope and arch bricks give the window an interesting shape

CLEVER CAROUSEL

This tower is box-shaped, with a window on one side just large enough for a minifigure to be seen. Check out that central turret... it functions as the turning handle for the carousel. Clever, huh?

Flaming wall torches highlight the window

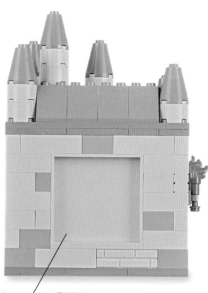

1×6×5 panels fill out the side walls

SIDE VIEW

SPECIAL PIECE

The 4×4 turntable base has a simple design but a very clever function. Click a round plate with hole on top of it and the plate will spin around freely.

6×6 round plate on the bottom mirrors the top

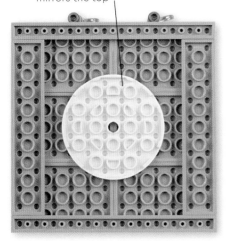

BOTTOM VIEW

This 2×2×2 cone spins

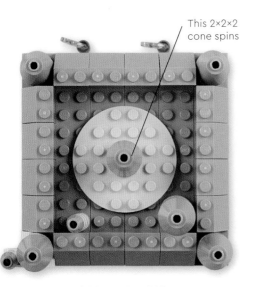

TOP VIEW

TAKE YOUR TURN

Underneath the carousel of minifigures is a hidden turntable base that allows it to spin. An axle rises up from the turntable all the way to the central castle tower, which controls the turning mechanism.

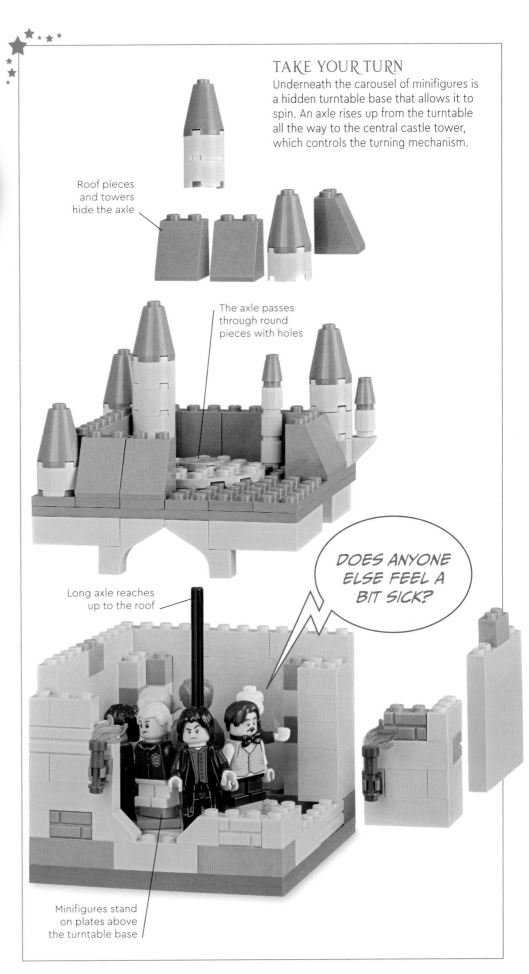

Roof pieces and towers hide the axle

The axle passes through round pieces with holes

Long axle reaches up to the roof

DOES ANYONE ELSE FEEL A BIT SICK?

Minifigures stand on plates above the turntable base

BLOCKY BRICK CHARACTERS

This blockbuster of a challenge is simple but clever. You and your friends build Harry Potter characters, then ask each other to guess who they are. Sounds easy? There's a catch. You can only use the simplest of bricks and plates to make them. Think carefully, and pick a recognizable character like Harry, a Death Eater, or even You-Know-Who. Can you guess who these characters are? Turn to pages 186–187 for the answers.

WHOOO DO YOU THINK WE ARE?

Snowy coloring

4

Transparent 1×2 brick is a pair of glasses

I

Long brown hair

2

Blue 2×2 plate hat

3

A 2×2 slope makes a good jaunty hat

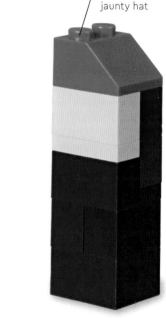

5

Pointy 1×1 slope ears

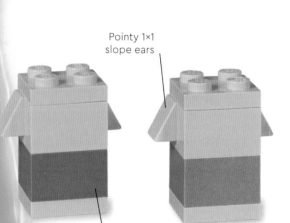

I THINK I KNOW THIS BLOCKHEAD.

6

Gray 2×2 brick rags

7

Red hair made from a 2×2 plate and 1×2 brick

8

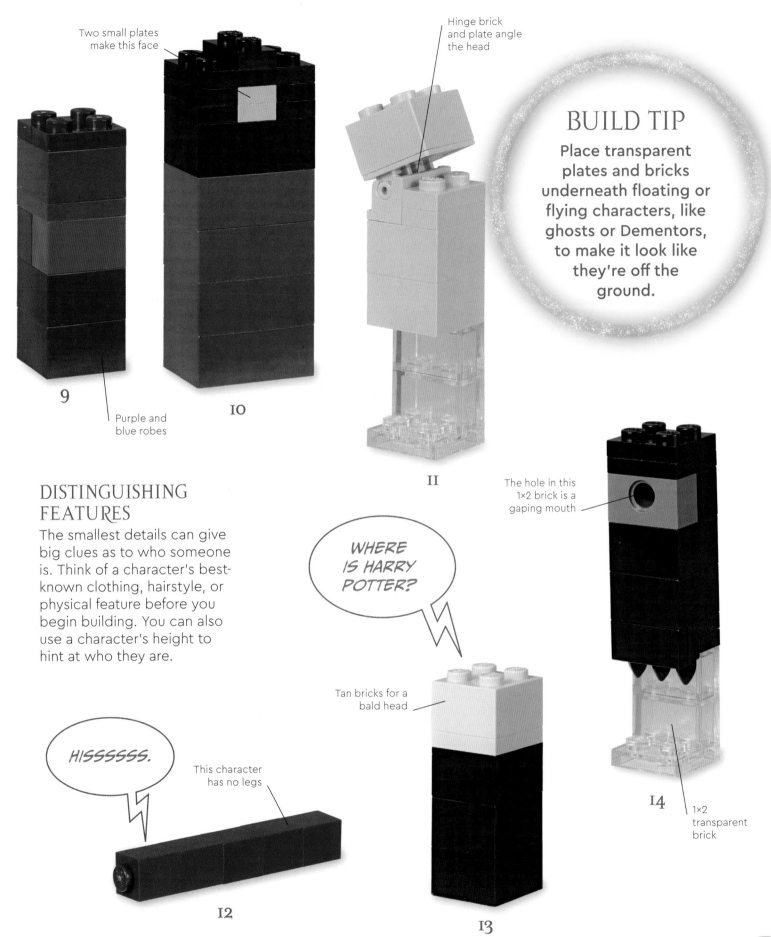

Two small plates make this face

Hinge brick and plate angle the head

BUILD TIP

Place transparent plates and bricks underneath floating or flying characters, like ghosts or Dementors, to make it look like they're off the ground.

9

Purple and blue robes

10

11

DISTINGUISHING FEATURES

The smallest details can give big clues as to who someone is. Think of a character's best-known clothing, hairstyle, or physical feature before you begin building. You can also use a character's height to hint at who they are.

WHERE IS HARRY POTTER?

The hole in this 1×2 brick is a gaping mouth

HISSSSSS.

This character has no legs

Tan bricks for a bald head

12

13

14

1×2 transparent brick

BUILD YOUR OWN PATRONUS

Expecto Patronum! Harry and his friends can summon their Patronus from the end of their wand. You might have to put in a bit more effort and build yours with LEGO bricks! What animal will you choose to be your silvery magical guardian? Try to pick something that represents your personality.

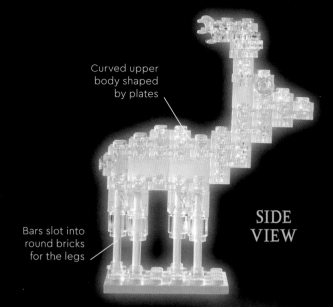

Curved upper body shaped by plates

Bars slot into round bricks for the legs

SIDE VIEW

Blue 1×1 round plate eyes stand out

Long snout for sniffing out danger

White base plate helps the deer stay upright

Stack up plates with clips at right angles for gnarly antlers

HARRY'S STAG
This staggeringly impressive build is Harry's Patronus... a stag. Unlike you, Harry didn't get to choose his own Patronus. It was magically decided for him. Maybe he got a stag because his dad had one as his Patronus, too.

ANTLER VIEW

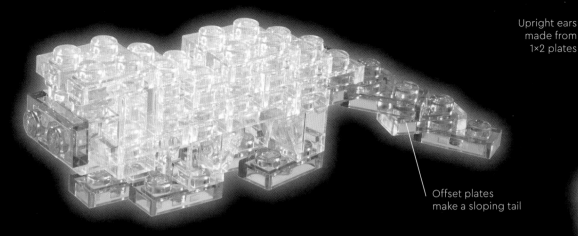

Offset plates
make a sloping tail

HERMIONE'S OTTER

Isn't this build otterly
brilliant? With that long,
tapering tail and short,
square feet, it can only be
Hermione's otter Patronus.

Blue pieces
highlight the feet,
tail, and nose

SIDE VIEW

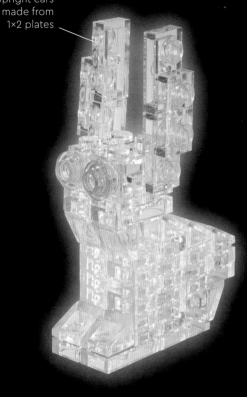

Upright ears
made from
1×2 plates

LUNA'S HARE

Did you know that the name Luna
means "moon"? Or that in some
myths, hares are associated with
the moon? This hare Patronus
definitely looks ready to spring
to Luna Lovegood's defense.

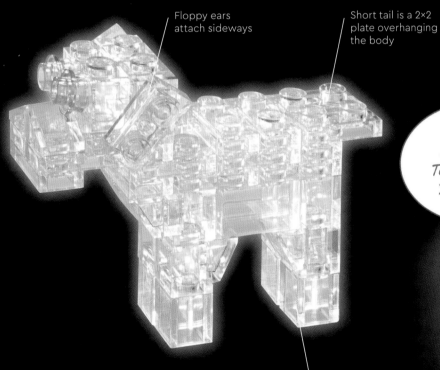

Floppy ears
attach sideways

Short tail is a 2×2
plate overhanging
the body

RON'S TERRIER

A Patronus doesn't have to be a be
a wild animal. Loyal, down-to-earth
Ron has a Jack Russell terrier as his.
Why not pick a family pet as your
Patronus, or another animal that
conjures up fond memories?

1×1 bricks
for paws

USE YOUR
PATRONUS
TO PROTECT
YOURSELF!

WIZARD SNAP

This card game will have you seeing double. It's the classic game Snap, of course, with a Harry Potter twist. Deal out a LEGO deck of cards featuring Hogwarts items, then be first to spot the matching pairs. There are two of every card in this game, but there can only be one winner. Now, snap to it!

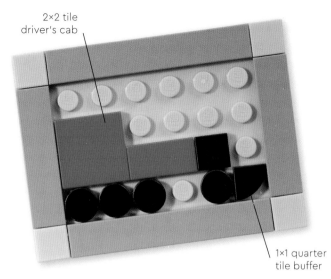

2×2 tile driver's cab

1×1 quarter tile buffer

HOGWARTS EXPRESS

CREATIVE CARDS

Part of the fun is deciding on images to decorate your cards. You could have magical vehicles, potion ingredients, animals, or a complete mix. Hogwarts cards can also be used for other simple card games.

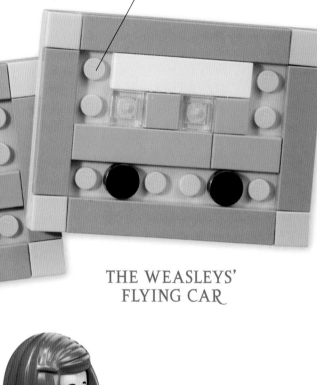

Each card is built on a 6×8 plate

THE WEASLEYS' FLYING CAR

1×4 tile roof

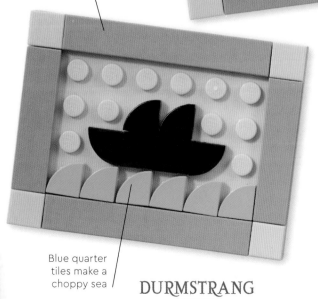

Line the card edges with tiles for a neat look

Blue quarter tiles make a choppy sea

DURMSTRANG SHIP

SNAP!

1. Build a deck of cards depicting Hogwarts-themed icons. There must be two matching cards for each item.

2. Turn the cards over, shuffle them, then deal out the same number of cards to each player.

3. Working in rounds, each player turns one of their cards face up and places it on a pile in the middle of all players.

4. The first to spot two matching face-up cards shouts "Snap!" They then claim the pile of cards and put them face down under their own cards.

5. Whoever ends up with all the cards is the Wizard Snap winner.

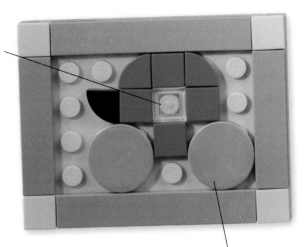

1×1 transparent tile window

BEAUXBATONS' CARRIAGE

Large carriage wheels are 2×2 round tiles

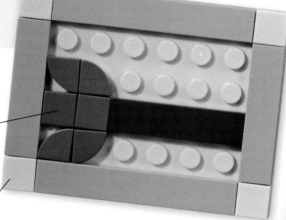

Lighter brown tiles are the bristles

If you don't have lots of tiles, use small plates instead

NIMBUS 2000

OH YEAH, WE'RE A PAIR OF JOKERS!

BUILD TIP

Use the same color plates and tiles for the back and sides of the cards so they look identical when flipped over. Otherwise, it will be too easy to remember which card is which.

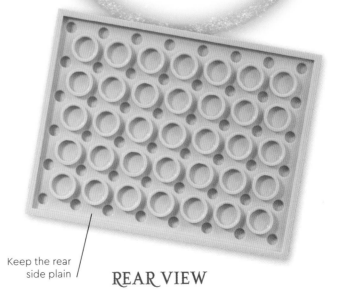

Keep the rear side plain

REAR VIEW

FIND THE KEY

Seven doorways. Seven flying keys. Harry's looking for the key to the middle door because behind it is a magical prize... the legendary Sorcerer's Stone! Challenge your friends to match the keys with the doors in this pairing game. The clues are in the blue elements above each doorway.

Make this part of each key (the "bit") unique

2×4 wedge plate is a fluttering wing

HOW TO PLAY

1 Taking turns, each player must select one key at a time and examine it, looking for a piece that matches a doorway clue.

2 When someone matches a key and door, they should put that key down in front of its door before the search continues.

3 Whichever player finds the key to the middle door first is the winner.

LEGO Technic axle connector with four bars fits into a brick with open stud

Give each key a handle or "bow" of your own design

YOU LOOK REALLY KEYED UP, HARRY!

1×1 brick with side stud

Brick-built wall topped with a tile

Three doors fit onto three 2×4 base plates

1

2

3

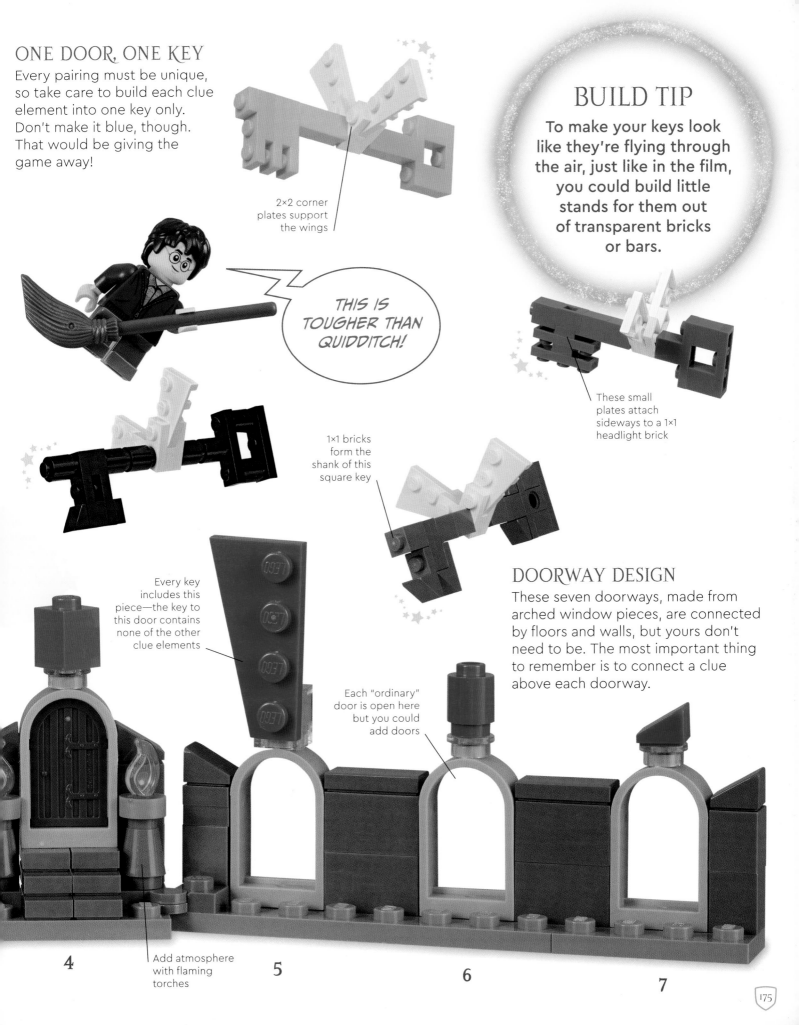

ONE DOOR, ONE KEY

Every pairing must be unique, so take care to build each clue element into one key only. Don't make it blue, though. That would be giving the game away!

2×2 corner plates support the wings

THIS IS TOUGHER THAN QUIDDITCH!

BUILD TIP

To make your keys look like they're flying through the air, just like in the film, you could build little stands for them out of transparent bricks or bars.

These small plates attach sideways to a 1×1 headlight brick

1×1 bricks form the shank of this square key

DOORWAY DESIGN

These seven doorways, made from arched window pieces, are connected by floors and walls, but yours don't need to be. The most important thing to remember is to connect a clue above each doorway.

Every key includes this piece—the key to this door contains none of the other clue elements

Each "ordinary" door is open here but you could add doors

4

Add atmosphere with flaming torches

5

6

7

PIN THE TAIL ON SCABBERS

Poor Scabbers. Ron's scruffy old pet rat seems to have lost his tail. Give him a replacement one in this fun game, doing your best to get it in the right place while blindfolded. There are lots of variations of this challenge you could build, like pinning the beak on Buckbeak or attaching a fang to the Basilisk (if you're feeling brave).

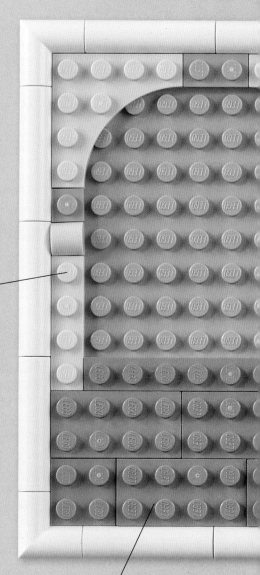

Tan plates suggest the hallways of Hogwarts

SPECIAL PIECE

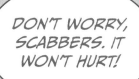

Scabbers' three sharp claws are all one piece. It was first used as a minifigure accessory for wolflike characters but it has many uses as a regular element.

THE BIG PICTURE

Increase your chances in this game by making Scabbers bigger and the background smaller. When you're ready to play, grab your tail element and do your best to find Scabbers' derrière!

Keep the background simple so players can't feel their way around!

DON'T WORRY, SCABBERS. IT WON'T HURT!

SQU-EEK!

HOW TO PLAY

1 Build a LEGO picture of Scabbers without his tail. The picture should be made up of mostly plates or bricks with their studs facing outward.

2 Look for a long piece, like a minifigure whip accessory, to use as the tail. If you don't have a whip, any long-shaped piece will do.

3 Players take turns to put on a blindfold, spin around three times, and then try to attach the tail to the right place.

4 The winner is the player who puts the tail nearest the right place on the picture.

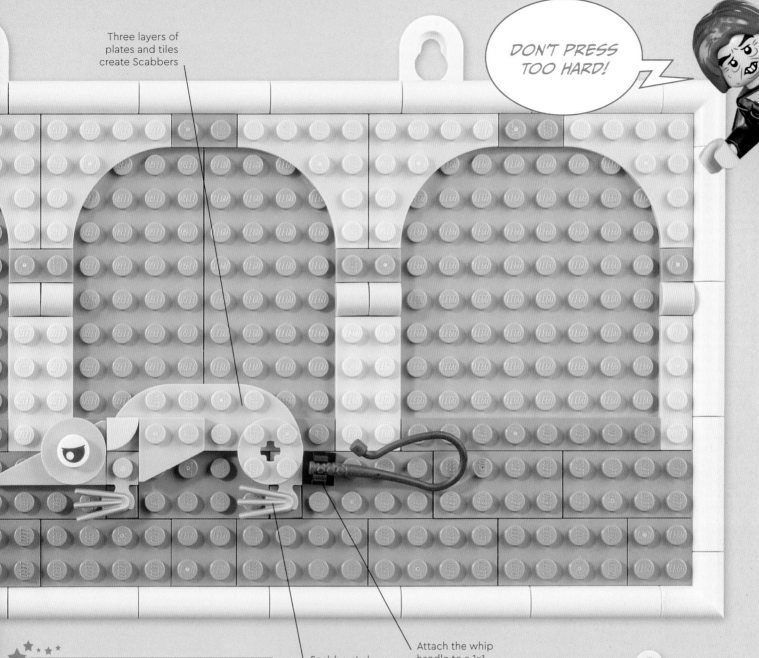

Three layers of plates and tiles create Scabbers

DON'T PRESS TOO HARD!

Scabbers' claws are held by a plate with clip

Attach the whip handle to a 1×1 tile with clip

HANG IT UP
Before you play with your picture, finish it off with a frame and add a couple of loop-shaped pieces at the top so you can hang the picture on a wall.

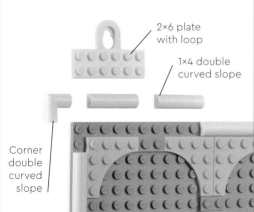

2×6 plate with loop

1×4 double curved slope

Corner double curved slope

ALTERNATIVE IDEA
Believe it or not, this picture is Scabbers too. It shows him after Ron almost—but not quite—turned him into a goblet in Transfiguration class. Scabbers' telltale tail was left growing out of the neck of the goblet.

This smaller picture uses the same building techniques

ESCAPE FROM GRINGOTTS

After rescuing a stolen item from Gringotts Bank, Harry, Ron, and Hermione discovered that breaking out of the super-secure building is harder than breaking in. Especially if Griphook the goblin betrays you! In this die-rolling game, you and a friend race to ride a dragon out of there before the building comes tumbling down.

HOW TO PLAY

1 Two players take turns to roll a die and move a LEGO minifigure forward.

2 If one player lands on a red square, the top floor of Gringotts is flipped over and play continues.

3 If the second player lands on a red square, the next floor of Gringotts is flipped over. The building collapses, and both players lose.

4 Players must roll the exact number on the die to reach the end. The first minifigure there hops on the dragon and escapes.

ON THE MOVE

The Ironbelly dragon has many moving parts connected to its body build. The wings attach to plates with bars, while the long neck moves up and down in two places thanks to click-hinge connections.

Hinge cylinder with axle holder

This axle connects the neck pieces

1×2 plate with bar

KEEP ROLLING ON

To increase the difficulty level of this game, make the board longer and add a few more red plates. Make sure your Ukrainian Ironbelly dragon is ready for takeoff at the end and that there's space onboard for a minifigure.

4×4 wedge plate wing

DON'T TOUCH THAT DRAGON!

Make a smooth tile plinth for the dragon to stand on

SPECIAL PIECE

The high-functioning 2×4 hinge plate can flip open and shut in a flash. As well as flipping great builds like this, you could use it for box lids or snapping jaws.

Don't make the building sections too heavy

6×8 plate makes a stable building base

FRONT (FLIPPED) VIEW

Stacked round bricks for pillars

HEY... JUMPING ON THE DRAGON WAS MY IDEA!

Smooth curved slopes hold each tower section at an angle

Watch out for the red game squares!

There are open doorways on each floor

REAR VIEW

179

SECRET DOORWAYS

Which secret door will magically open when pushed? This guessing game is simple but fun. Make it harder by having three doors and two doorstops, or pick a different door theme. You could have a row of doors that all open, but only one has a LEGO piece "reward" behind it.

1×6×2 arches shape the tops of the alcoves

A tall chest of drawers fits inside this alcove

Torches attach to 1×1 bricks with clips in the walls

Include potion bottles for a Hogwarts feel

I'M A GHOST. CAN'T I JUST FLOAT THROUGH?

DOORS IN DISGUISE

This is Hogwarts, remember. Ordinary doors just won't do. Keep to the theme and disguise your doors as alcoves in an old passageway, complete with furniture.

SPECIAL PIECE

The hinge bricks that the doors in this game swing on come in two parts. The top section slots into the bottom part so the two bricks can move together.

SECRET STUDS

Hidden inside this smooth-looking wall are lots of hardworking bricks with side studs. Those at the top of the wall hold tiles that make the ceiling look carved or vaulted.

2×3 pentagonal tile

1×4 brick with side studs

REAR VIEW (CLOSED)

This gap could hold the red brick on the next round

NO PEEKING AT THE BACK!

The top of the wall is two studs wide

Torch base is a faucet element

SIDE VIEW

Each door is one stud wide

1×2 hinge bricks let the doors open and close

1×2 brick doorstop

This cabinet attaches to sideways studs on the door

REAR VIEW (OPEN)

SPOT THE GRIM

There's a real stir in Professor Trelawney's Divination class when the teacher spies a sign called "the Grim"—a spectral dog that is said to bring doom—at the bottom of Harry's teacup. In this game, you and your friends race to build your interpretation of the Grim from LEGO tea leaves. What will the winner's prize be? A nice cup of tea, perhaps!

Plates with petals make a flower-patterned teacup

1×1 headlight bricks hold both ends of this handle

CUPPA, ANYONE?

Create some 2D teacups as decorative accessories to hide your Grim picture behind as you build. Or try building larger, 3D ones to put the tea leaves inside.

OH NO... YOU'VE GOT THE GRIM, HARRY!

This minifigure whip accessory could be useful

Minifigure bucket handle—anything will do!

HOW TO PLAY

1 Give each friend a selection of small, brown LEGO elements to represent tea leaves.

2 Set a timer for three minutes and ask players to form a picture of the Grim with the tea leaves. It could be the whole animal, a worried face, or something else entirely.

3 When time is up, everyone reveals their pictures to the group.

4 The winner is the player who everyone agrees has come up with the eeriest Grim.

1×1 round plates form the Grim's body

THE GRIM 1 (SNARLING DOG)

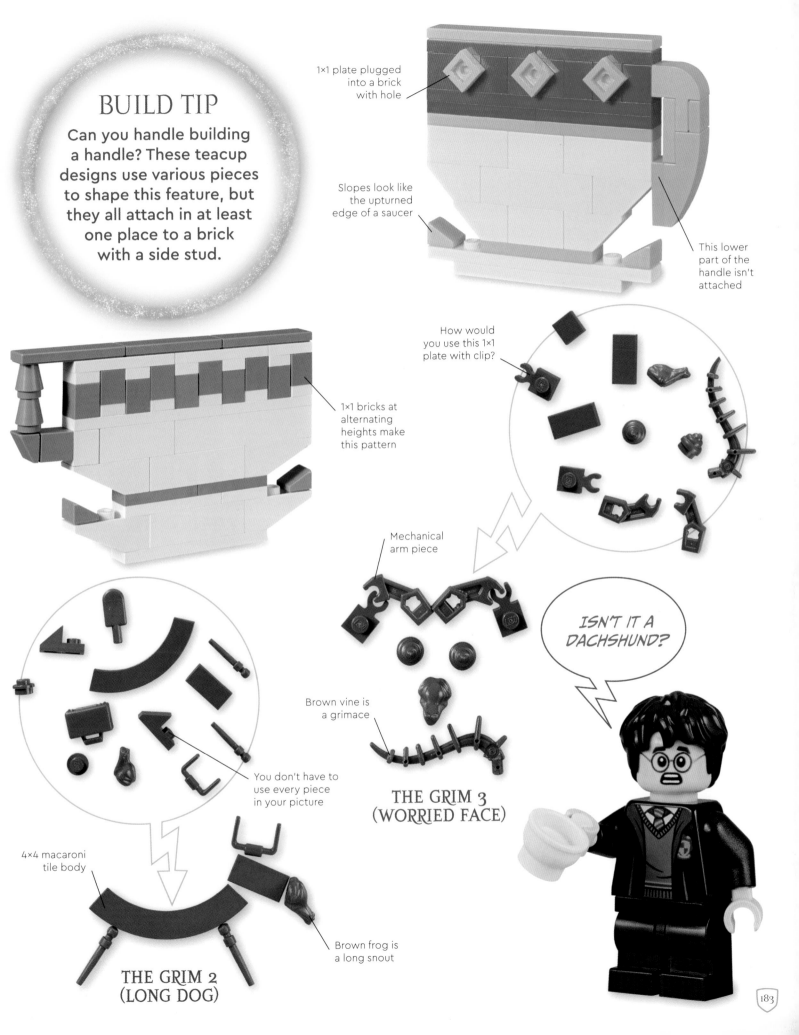

BUILD TIP

Can you handle building a handle? These teacup designs use various pieces to shape this feature, but they all attach in at least one place to a brick with a side stud.

1×1 plate plugged into a brick with hole

Slopes look like the upturned edge of a saucer

This lower part of the handle isn't attached

1×1 bricks at alternating heights make this pattern

How would you use this 1×1 plate with clip?

Mechanical arm piece

Brown vine is a grimace

ISN'T IT A DACHSHUND?

You don't have to use every piece in your picture

THE GRIM 3 (WORRIED FACE)

4×4 macaroni tile body

Brown frog is a long snout

THE GRIM 2 (LONG DOG)

183

OBLIVIATE!

You won't forget this LEGO card game in a hurry! It's based on the Forgetfulness Charm in the Harry Potter movies, which erases memories from people's minds. In this case, it's a little black Obliviate card that will mess with your memory. Hold that thought, and start building.

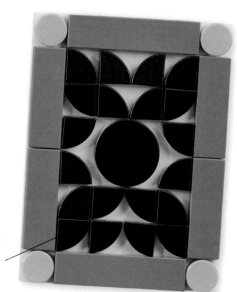

Black tiles suggest a memory blackout

OBLIVIATE CARD

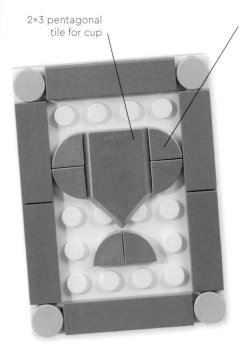

2×3 pentagonal tile for cup

Don't have gold tiles? Make your cup silvery gray or a bright color

TRIWIZARD CUP

MARK YOUR CARDS

The "enchanting" Obliviate card should stand out from the colorful pair cards. This game's Obliviate card has a pattern that looks like a puff of black smoke. Make all the card backs plain, so they can't be identified when face down.

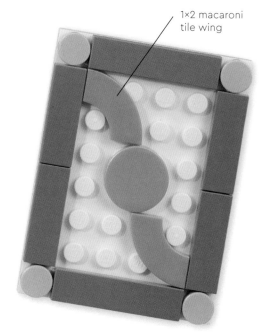

1×2 macaroni tile wing

GOLDEN SNITCH

COME LAST AGAIN, VOLDEMORT?

White 6×8 plate base

REAR VIEW

HOW TO PLAY

1. Use LEGO bricks to build a deck of Harry Potter-themed cards. There must be two of each picture card, but only one Obliviate card.

2. Turn the cards face down, shuffle them, and lay them flat on the floor or a table.

3. Players take turns to pick two cards. If a matching pair is revealed, the player wins those cards. If the two cards don't match, they are turned face down again.

4. When someone turns over the Obliviate card, all remaining cards in the game are reshuffled and then laid down in a different position.

5. The game ends when only the Obliviate card remains. The player who has collected the most pairs is the winner.

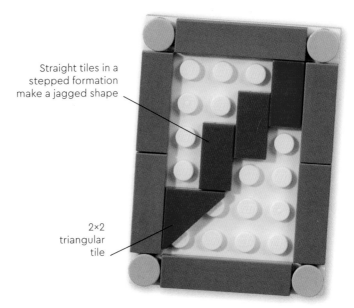

Straight tiles in a stepped formation make a jagged shape

2×2 triangular tile

HARRY'S SCAR

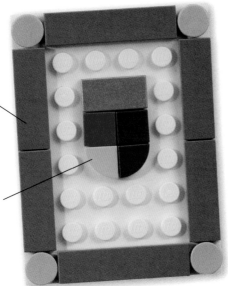

The same color tiles line the edge of each card

Colors represent each Hogwarts house

HOGWARTS CREST

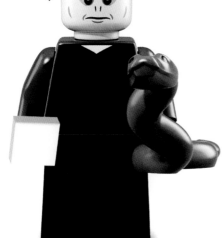

FORGET IT!

BUILD TIP
Printed eye tiles are very useful if you like to build animals and other creatures. There are all kinds —winking, fierce, smiley— so you can give your creations lots of personality.

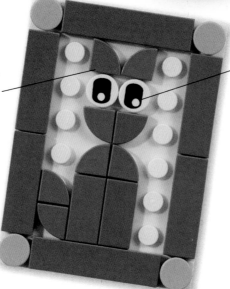

1×1 quarter tile ears

1×1 narrow eye tile

PROFESSOR MCGONAGALL AS A CAT

SOLUTIONS

PAGES 148-149: TRIWIZARD MAZE

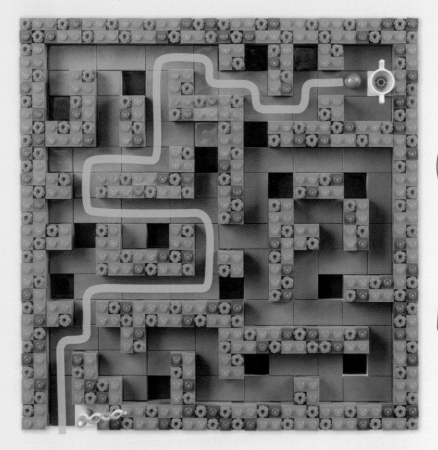

IF YOU CAN'T REACH THE CUP, YOU CAN HAVE THIS ONE!

PAGES 174-175: FIND THE KEY

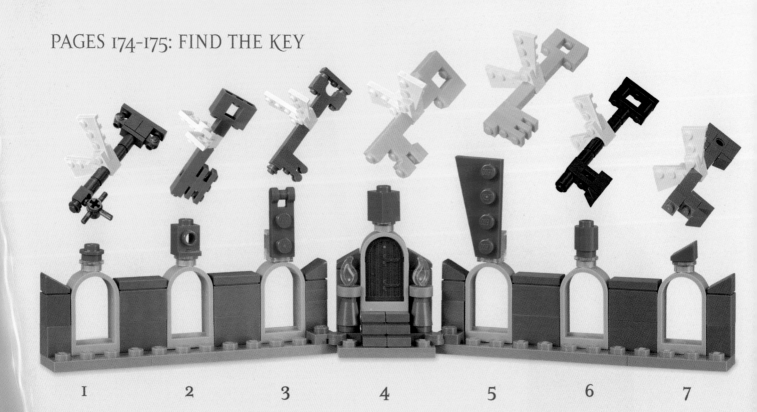

1   2   3   4   5   6   7

1. HARRY
POTTER

2. HERMIONE
GRANGER

3. PROFESSOR
DUMBLEDORE

4. HEDWIG

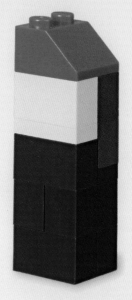

5. PROFESSOR
MCGONAGALL

6. KREACHER

7. DOBBY

8. RON
WEASLEY

9. KINGSLEY
SHACKLEBOLT

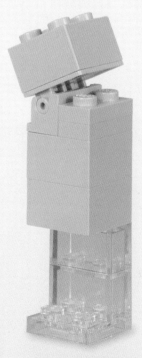

13. LORD
VOLDEMORT

10. RUBEUS
HAGRID

11. NEARLY
HEADLESS
NICK

12. NAGINI

14. DEMENTOR

187

MEET THE BUILDERS

JESSICA FARRELL

WHICH MODEL OF YOURS IN THIS BOOK IS YOUR FAVORITE?

I'm quite fond of the wizard desk caddies (pages 132–133). They are examples of how simple, practical objects can be artistic yet useful. They are just the sort of thing you might find in the wizarding world.

HOW MUCH RESEARCH DID YOU DO BEFORE BUILDING YOUR HARRY POTTER MODELS? WHAT PARTICULARLY INSPIRED YOU?

I've read all the books and watched all the films several times, so I was already a fan! For this book, I studied a lot of film clips, searching for little details and determining the mood in each scene.

WHAT TIPS DO YOU HAVE FOR BUILDING LEGO® HARRY POTTER™ MODELS?

Look at historical buildings and things in museums for inspiration. Natural, earthy colors may work better than bright ones when trying to get the right "feel."

BUILDER BIO
Location:
County Kildare, Ireland
Day job:
LEGO artist
LEGO speciality: Architecture, art, and organic forms
Favorite Harry Potter character:
Professor Severus Snape

WHICH LEGO ELEMENTS DO YOU USE MOST IN YOUR BUILDS?

The jumper plate has always featured most often in my models because it allows for fine detailing, but recently I've been using the 1×2 curved slope even more frequently. This slope is really useful for creating the natural curves of animals and plants. It has become my new favorite!

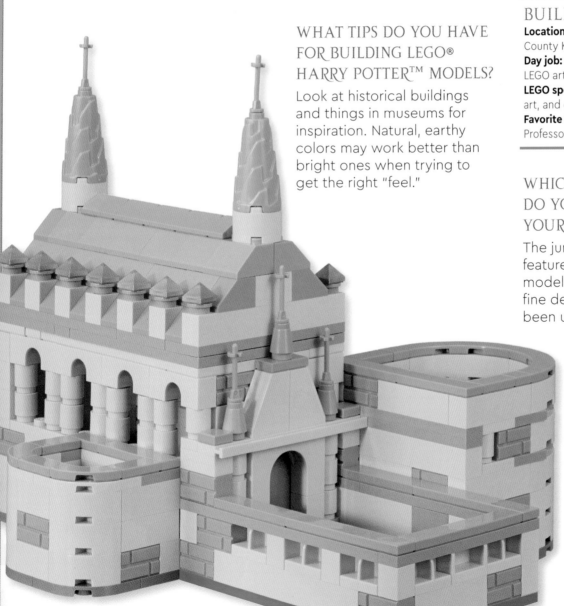

JESSICA'S HOGWARTS DESK CADDY, PAGE 132

WHAT DO YOU MOST LOVE ABOUT BUILDING LEGO HARRY POTTER MODELS?

The wizarding world is full of magical mystery and fantasy; getting the chance to re-create some of it in brick form was great fun. I could even imagine I was part of the story!

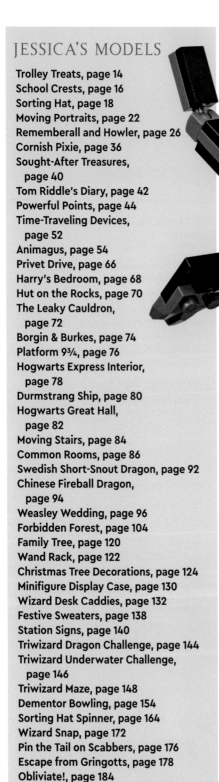

JESSICA'S PADFOOT,
PAGE 55

DID YOU PLAN OUT YOUR BUILDS FOR THIS BOOK?

There's always lots of research for me to do before starting a new model, but I don't really plan things out after that. Instead of drawing plans on paper or a computer, I imagine how I'd like the model to look and I design and redesign it in my mind. I do this so many times that it often feels like I've finished the model before I even start!

DID ANY OF THE MODELS IN THIS BOOK NOT GO ACCORDING TO PLAN OR PROVE TRICKIER TO BUILD THAN ANTICIPATED?

Many times I thought I'd designed something exactly right, only to discover a key element was not available in the color I wanted to use. Color is really important to me, so if I couldn't find a good substitute piece, I ended up redesigning the whole model!

DO YOU HAVE A TOP LEGO BUILDING TIP?

This tip is from a good friend, who is a LEGO set designer: whenever you come across a new LEGO element, fiddle around with it and see how it connects with other pieces; try it out in a mini model. This way, you'll remember the element at a time when you may need it.

ALEXANDER BLAIS

WHICH MODEL OF YOURS IN THIS BOOK IS YOUR FAVORITE?

I'm most proud of my Marauder's Map (pages 46–47) because it is the largest of my models and one of the most complicated. I'm also very fond of my rat (page 117) because it's simple yet so expressive.

WHAT RESEARCH DID YOU DO BEFORE BUILDING YOUR HARRY POTTER MODELS? WHAT PARTICULARLY INSPIRED YOU?

I've read the books and seen the movies tons of times, but I wanted to immerse myself in the stories again for this book. While I was building, I was always either watching the movies in the background or listening to the audio books. I also found a lot of reference images online to help me get things right.

WHICH LEGO® ELEMENT IS YOUR FAVORITE?

I really like the 1×2 jumper plate. Despite its deceptively simple design, it can be used in so many different ways. It allows you to offset (place out of line) pieces by half a brick, so you can make realistic shapes.

BUILDER BIO

Location:
Ebeltoft, Denmark
Day job:
Film student
LEGO speciality: Small details and realism
Favorite Harry Potter character: Professor Albus Dumbledore

DID YOU PLAN OUT YOUR BUILDS FOR THIS BOOK?

I found reference images to base each model on and sometimes made a sketch or two to make sure I understood what I was building. But, mostly, I would take a box of elements and start putting them together to see what I came up with. I like to be inspired by the pieces I have.

ALEXANDER'S MODELS

DID YOU LEARN ANY NEW BUILDING TECHNIQUES FOR THIS BOOK?

For my Mysterious Bathroom (pages 88–89) washbasin build I had to figure out how to create something with six sides. I had not tried this before, but I think it turned out well!

ALEXANDER'S BATHROOM SINK, PAGE 88

ROD GILLIES

WHICH MODEL OF YOURS IN THIS BOOK IS YOUR FAVORITE?

It has to be my microscale Hogwarts Express (page 109). I was delighted to be able to get that level of detail into such a small footprint. I was also particularly pleased with the arches in the station walls.

WHAT RESEARCH DID YOU DO BEFORE BUILDING YOUR HARRY POTTER MODELS? WHAT PARTICULARLY INSPIRED YOU?

I looked up lots of pictures online and rewatched a couple of the films. I also took a good look at the official LEGO® Harry Potter™ sets to make sure I wasn't building something in the same way as it had been done before—I really wanted my models to offer some new inspiration.

WHICH LEGO ELEMENT IS YOUR FAVORITE?

I love a 1×1 headlight brick. It's so versatile and helps you make really interesting shapes.

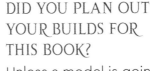

DID YOU PLAN OUT YOUR BUILDS FOR THIS BOOK?

Unless a model is going to end up at a large size, I tend not to plan too much. I much prefer to sit down and start fiddling with bricks. I find it much more fun to just see what happens rather than planning everything out.

BUILDER BIO

Location:
Edinburgh, Scotland
Day job:
Marketer and innovator
LEGO speciality: Microscale
Favorite Harry Potter character:
Professor Severus Snape

ROD'S MODELS

Founders' Items, page 20
Boggart Cabinet, page 34
Secret Passages, page 102
Microscale Hogwarts,
 page 106
Microscale Scenes,
 page 108
Camping Out, page 110
Book Nook, page 128
Deck the Hall, page 158
Secret Doorways, page 180

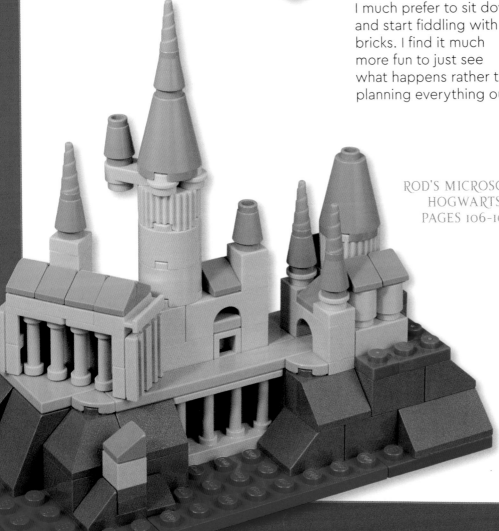

ROD'S MICROSCALE HOGWARTS, PAGES 106-107

DID ANY OF THE MODELS IN THIS BOOK PROVE TRICKER THAN ANTICIPATED?

The microscale models are always tricky. There's a lot of work that goes into making something look so simple. I must have built and rebuilt those models dozens of times, always trying to make them a little tighter and smaller with each new version.

BARNEY MAIN

WHICH MODEL OF YOURS IN THIS BOOK IS YOUR FAVORITE?

I love the Pick a Potion game (pages 152–153). There's hardly any building involved, but it uses lots of imagination and fun elements. The game shows just how versatile a toy LEGO® pieces can be.

WHAT TIPS DO YOU HAVE FOR BUILDING LEGO® HARRY POTTER™ MODELS?

Use the colors from the four Hogwarts houses in stripes or checkerboard patterns. They make objects and scenes instantly recognizable and also stop models from looking entirely brown, black, and gray.

DID ANY OF THE HARRY POTTER BUILDS IN THIS BOOK NOT GO ACCORDING TO PLAN OR PROVE TRICKIER TO BUILD THAN ANTICIPATED?

The Tabletop Quidditch game (pages 150–151) was tricky, as it's a difficult game to play without magic! I did lots of experimenting with different ways to throw and shoot the balls. The Golden Snitch shooter was particularly difficult. The best way to work out that kind of mechanism is to build a very rough model where you can change lots of things (e.g. the height of the tower or the size of the catapult) to work out the best layout. You can worry about making it look nice later!

WHAT DO YOU MOST LOVE ABOUT BUILDING HARRY POTTER MODELS?

There's such a large and recognizable universe to draw from. I could have built hundreds of characters for the Blocky Brick Characters challenge (pages 168–169). I loved making Nearly Headless Nick's defining characteristic from just a hinge brick and plate!

IF YOU COULD DESIGN A NEW HARRY POTTER SET FOR THE LEGO GROUP, WHAT WOULD IT BE?

It would be cool to create the full set of obstacles guarding the Sorcerer's Stone in Hogwarts' Underground Chambers (the Devil's Snare plants, wizard's chess, flying keys, etc). The builder could play their way through the tasks.

BUILDER BIO

Location:
Swindon, UK
Day job:
Design engineer
LEGO speciality: Inventing games, tricks, and challenges
Favorite Harry Potter character:
Remus Lupin

BARNEY'S WEASLEY FAMILY CLOCK, PAGES 118-119

BARNEY'S MODELS

MARIANN ASANUMA

WHICH MODEL OF YOURS IN THIS BOOK IS YOUR FAVORITE?

Probably the mini Quidditch stadium (page 91). I love how it came out, especially the tiny brooms made from the new chopsticks element.

DID YOU PLAN OUT YOUR BUILDS FOR THIS BOOK?

I do to some extent. When I know what I am planning to build, such as Hermione's magic bag (see below), I look at reference photos of the real item and try to figure out how to re-create it in LEGO® pieces. That model was a particularly tricky one because it is a drawstring purse. Getting it right took several attempts and I had to try out many different techniques before I was happy with it.

DO YOU HAVE A FAVORITE BUILDING TECHNIQUE THAT YOU USE ALL THE TIME?

I love to use SNOT ("studs not on top") techniques, where you attach pieces sideways. I used lots of SNOT building on the World Cup Quidditch case (page 90), for example.

IF YOU HAD ALL THE TIME IN THE WORLD, WHAT HARRY POTTER MODEL OF YOUR OWN DESIGN WOULD YOU BUILD?

I would love to make a life-size version of the mermaid stained-glass window that you see in *Harry Potter and the Goblet of Fire* (2005). It appears when Harry is figuring out the Triwizard Tournament riddle in the bathtub.

BUILDER BIO

Location:
Salt Lake City, Utah
Day job:
LEGO artist
LEGO speciality: Microscale
Favorite Harry Potter character:
Nymphadora Tonks

MARIANN'S MODELS

Great Hall Feast, page 24
The Weasley's Kitchen Items, page 50
Magic Bag, page 58
World Cup Quidditch, page 90
Magical Newspaper, page 134
Tower of Treats, page 156
Make a Muggle Item Magical, page 160
Build Your Own Patronus, page 170

MARIANN'S
MAGIC BAG,
PAGES 58-59

WHAT DO YOU MOST LOVE ABOUT BUILDING LEGO® HARRY POTTER™ MODELS?

The variety of models that I got to make. I created models in microscale, minifigure scale, and life-size for this project.

NATE DIAS

WHAT RESEARCH DID YOU DO BEFORE BUILDING YOUR HARRY POTTER MODELS? WHAT PARTICULARLY INSPIRED YOU?

I loved the Harry Potter films and books growing up, and I even went to a midnight premiere of *Harry Potter and the Deathly Hallows* (2010). For this book, I did a lot of research online to get the right look for my models, especially my Wizard Wheezes (pages 48–49).

WHICH LEGO® ELEMENT IS YOUR FAVORITE?

It has to be the 1×2 plate. Yes, it's a very ordinary element, but a 1×2 plate is capable of becoming almost any other brick when you have a lot of them. It is also the smallest element that you can start building something 3D with.

DID YOU PLAN OUT YOUR BUILDS FOR THIS BOOK?

I planned all of my builds for this book on a computer. Building digitally really helps me to be creative as I can use any LEGO pieces I want—even if I don't have them in my collection yet.

DO YOU HAVE A TOP LEGO BUILDING TIP?

My top tip for all budding builders is just to start building. If you have an idea in your head, give building it a try. You may surprise yourself with the outcome.

BUILDER BIO

Location:
Nottinghamshire, UK
Day job:
Science teacher
LEGO speciality: Animals and real-world objects
Favorite Harry Potter character:
Mad-Eye Moody

IF YOU COULD DESIGN A NEW HARRY POTTER SET FOR THE LEGO GROUP, WHAT WOULD IT BE?

It would have to be the vaults of Gringotts Wizarding Bank. The set would feature a cool rollercoaster with goblins controlling the carriages, complete with an Ironbelly dragon and heaps of gold!

NATE'S WANTED POSTER, PAGES 62–63

NATE'S MODELS

BRICK TYPES

It doesn't take a wise witch or wizard to know that there are many different kinds of LEGO® pieces, but what are they all called and why? And what are they particularly useful for? If you want to become a brick expert, these pages will help you to better get to know some of the pieces in your LEGO collection.

Small parts and small balls can cause choking if swallowed. Not for children under 3 years.

MEASUREMENTS

The size of a LEGO piece is described by the number of studs it has. For example, a brick that has two studs along and three studs up is called a 2×3 brick. Tall parts have a third number, which is the height of the piece in standard bricks.

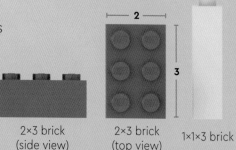

2×3 brick (side view)

2×3 brick (top view)

1×1×3 brick

1×2 jumper plate   2×2 jumper plate

JUMPER PLATES

These plates have only one stud in the middle, but they follow the same measurement system as standard plates. Jumper plates let you "jump" the usual grid of LEGO studs. They are useful for centering things in your models.

BRICKS

Where would builders be without this essential element? Bricks are the basis of most builds. They come in many shapes, sizes, and colors.

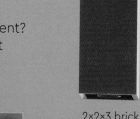

2×2×3 brick

1×2 ridged brick

2×2 round brick

2×2 corner brick

1×2 textured (masonry) brick

TILES

Tiles have tubes on the bottom but no studs on top. They can give your builds a smooth finish, while printed tiles can add interesting details to your models.

1×2 transparent tile

2×2 printed tile

2×2 round tile

1×4 tile

PLATES

Plates are similar to bricks. They have studs on top and tubes on the bottom, but plates are thinner. Three stacked plates are the same height as one standard brick.

4×4 round corner plate

Three 1×2 plates

1×2 brick

2×3 curved plate with hole

THERE ARE MORE PIECE TYPES THAN THERE ARE BOOKS IN HOGWARTS!

SIDE STUDS

If you want to build in multiple directions, choose a piece with studs on more than one side. These parts let you build upward as well as outward.

1×4/1×2 bracket plate

1×1 brick with one side stud

1×1 headlight brick

1×1 brick with four side studs

1×2/2×2 bracket plate (side view)

SLOPES

Slope bricks have diagonal angles. They come in many sizes and they can be curved or inverted (upside down).

1×2 slope brick

1×2 inverted slope brick

1×3 curved slope

CLIPS

Pieces with clips can attach to other elements, such as bars.

1×2 plate with clip

1×1 plate with clip

  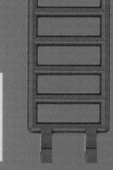

1×2 plate with two clips

1×1 tile with clip

2×3 tile with two clips

3×7 ladder with two clips

HINGES

You can add different types of motion to your builds with hinge pieces. Adding hinge plates and hinge bricks to your models will allow them to move from side to side or to tilt up and down.

Two 1×2 hinge plates

1×2 hinge brick with 2×2 hinge plate

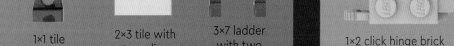

1×2 click hinge brick (top view)

1×2 hinge brick with 1×2 hinge plate (top view)

BARS

These long, thin pieces are just the right size to fit in a minifigure's hand. They can also be used with clips to add movement to your builds.

1×1 round plate with bar

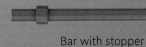

Bar with stopper

1×2 plate with bar

JOINTS

Plates and bricks with balls and sockets can make flexible, movable connections on your builds.

1×2 plate with tow ball

1×2 plate with ball socket

2×2 brick with two balls

LEGO® TECHNIC

These eclectic elements expand the range of functions you can build into your models. They are particularly useful for builds with lots of moving parts or technical details.

Friction pin

Axle

Axle pin

1×2 brick with axle hole

1×2×1⅔ pin connector plate with two holes

Axle connector

Axle with ball joint

1×3 beam

Axle and pin connector

Angled axle and pin connector

MAGICAL PIECES

1×4 wave flag

Owl

2×3 book

1×1 jewel

Broom

Candle flame

1×1 rock crystal

2×2×1⅓ dome top

Lantern

Goblet

Bat

Candle

Wand

Candlestick

Spider web with clips

Curly plant stem

SQUEAK!

Mouse

Treasure chest

Witch/wizard hat

Potion bottle

Small pot

Cauldron

USEFUL PIECES

Gather up your most enchanting LEGO® elements to create Harry Potter-themed models, and also look for pieces that could make fascinating creatures, crumbling buildings, overgrown plants, and towering trees. Don't worry if you don't have any of these pieces—just get creative with the ones you have.

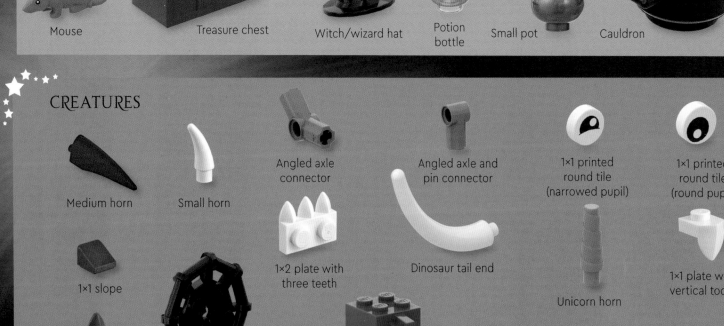

CREATURES

Medium horn

Small horn

Angled axle connector

Angled axle and pin connector

1×1 printed round tile (narrowed pupil)

1×1 printed round tile (round pupil)

1×2 plate with three teeth

Dinosaur tail end

Unicorn horn

1×1 slope

1×1 plate with vertical tooth

1×1 plate with horizontal tooth

2×2 round plate with octagonal bar

2×2 brick with click hinge finger

Click hinge cylinder with axle hole

1×2 rounded plate

Mechanical claw

OLD BUILDINGS

1×4×6 rounded door

1×2 log brick

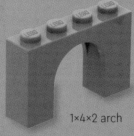

1×1 brick with scroll

1×6 raised arch

1×1 cone

1×4×2 ornamental lattice fence

1×4×2 arch

1×2×2⅔ rounded window

2×2×3 jagged cone

Telescope

1×4×5 wall with window

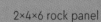

1×3×2 arch

2×3 pentagonal tile

2×4×6 rock panel

1×1 round tile with bar

Ski pole

PLANTS AND TREES

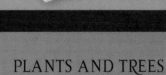

5×6 plant leaf

2×2 ridged round brick

Seaweed

Palm-tree top

Plant stem with three leaves

5×6 swordleaf plant

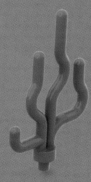

Plant stem

Four-scoop ice cream

1×1 round plate with three leaves

Flower stem with six stems

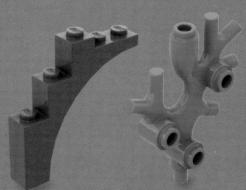

1×5×4 arch

Coral

2×2×4 prickly bush

Senior Editor Laura Palosuo
Project Art Editor Jenny Edwards
Production Editor Marc Staples
Senior Production Controller Lloyd Robertson
Managing Editor Paula Regan
Managing Art Editor Jo Connor
Publishing Director Mark Searle

Packaged for DK by Plum Jam
Editor Hannah Dolan **Designer** Guy Harvey

Inspirational models built by
Jessica Farrell, Alexander Blais, Rod Gillies,
Barney Main, Mariann Asanuma, and Nate Dias

Photography by Gary Ombler

Cover design by Jenny Edwards

Dorling Kindersley and Plum Jam would like to thank:
Randi Sørensen, Heidi K. Jensen, Martin Leighton Lindhart, and
Nina Koopman at the LEGO Group; Kurtis Estes, Victoria Selover,
and Katie Campbell at Warner Bros. Discovery, and Luke Barnard at
the Blair Partnership; Becky Smith for the use of her minifigure
collection; Victoria Taylor and Lara Hutcheson for editorial
assistance; Toby Truphet for design assistance; Elizabeth Dowsett
for proofreading; and Megan Douglass for Americanizing.

First American Edition, 2023
Published in the United States by DK Publishing
1745 Broadway, 20th Floor, New York NY 10019

Page design copyright © 2023 Dorling Kindersley Limited
DK, a division of Penguin Random House LLC
23 24 25 26 27 10 9 8 7 6 5 4 3 2 1
001–334770–Sep/2023

Manufactured by Dorling Kindersley,
One Embassy Gardens,
8 Viaduct Gardens, London SW11 7BW
under license from the LEGO Group.